9781935202356

W0017843

Design Miami/ 2012

Welcome to Design Miami/ 2012

Welcome to Design Miami/ 2012, the global forum for collectible design. December's fair presents masterworks from the twentieth century until today from the world's most influential design galleries alongside a progressive program of Satellite exhibitions, Design Talks and the prestigious Designer of the Year Award, presented to Acconci Studio. At the core of the Design Miami/ forum is the gallery program, which has evolved to encompass a strategic selection of galleries from around the globe with distinct areas of expertise. Each gallery selected to participate in the fair is chosen for its efforts to develop a comprehensive appreciation of movements, designers and individual works that have shaped design history.

Within it's roster of twenty-nine galleries, Design Miami/ welcomes six new exhibitors: Gabrielle Ammann // Gallery from Cologne, Galleria Rossella Colombari from Milan, Galerie BSL from Paris, Galerie Jacques Lacoste from Paris, Jason Jacques from New York and Moderne Gallery from Philadelphia. These galleries increase the fair's diversity of exhibitions, adding to the program Contemporary design from India and Germany, Historic Italian design, emerging French Contemporary design, the work of Jean Royére and American Studio Craft.

These galleries join returning exhibitors such as: Carpenters Workshop Gallery, Demisch Danant, Galerie Downtown-François Laffanour, Galerie kreo, Galerie Patrick Seguin, Galerie Pierre Marie Giraud, Hostler Burrows, Johnson Trading Gallery, Jousse Entreprise, Nilufar Gallery, R 20th Century, Priveekollektie, Gallery SEOMI and Galerie VIVID.

Complementing the main gallery shows, Design Miami's Design On/Site Galleries provides a space for experimentation and launches new work in installation-driven solo shows. Each On/Site expresses a distinct environment while providing collectors with exclusive access to fresh material.

This year's participants include Antonella Villanova presenting Delfina Delettrez, Booo presenting Front, Design Space presenting Michal Cederbaum and Noam Dover, Erastudio Apartment-Gallery presenting Gaetano Pesce, Mondo Cane presenting RO/LU, Victor Hunt Designart Dealer presenting Sylvain Willenz and Volume Gallery presenting Snarkitecture.

In addition to the gallery and On/Site exhibitions, Design Miami/ offers a diverse program of Satellite shows, Design Talks and the Designer of the Year Award. The Cooper-Hewitt National Design Museum and DAP/ ARTBOOK collaborate to present a pop-up shop of designed objects and publications reflecting designers and movements represented in the fair's exhibition program. Kenya Hara presents his Architecture for Dogs launch in the Miami Design District. Olfactive branding firm 12.29 scents the fair with Belle Isle, a sensory experience developed exclusively for Design Miami/. And Visitors to the fair will be greeted by Drift, an entrance pavilion by NY-based collaborative architectural studio Snarkitecture designed to mystify perceptions of volume and space through a suspended topography of massive inflatable tubes.

The 2012 Design Talks program continues to explore compelling topics in the design world. Three headline talks focus on Design Pioneers such as Diane Von Furstenberg and Vito Acconci, influential creatives in the world of fashion, architecture and design, who have shaped design history through their innovative approach.

In partnership with BE OPEN, a global initiative to foster innovation and creativity, Design Miami/ will launch the BE OPEN Forum. This series of profile talks with advanced thinkers will provide a unique portal into the intellectual curiosity of today's design minds.

This December's Designer of the Year Award has been presented to Acconci Studio for its acute and steadfast interest in generating unexpected and intense interactions, and in actively engaging both people and public places to explore the spectrum of human response. Since the 1980s, Acconci Studio has worked to challenge traditional approaches to design through innovative concepts and projects, many unrealized. Design Miami/, through the support of the Miami Design District, is honored to bring to life Acconci Studio's Klein Bottle Playground and to install a temporary exhibition during the week of the fair that illustrates the language of the studio to an international audience of art and design enthusiasts. Finally, Design Miami/ would not be possible without the generous support of our sponsors.

This December, the fair's primary supporters will launch an impressive selection of designed installations commissioned specially for Design Miami/. Exclusive Automotive Sponsor Audi presents a public lounge and exhibition of the R18 Ultra Chair conceived by designers Kram/ Weisshaar and developed using methods borrowed from the future of automotive manufacturing in collaboration with Audi's Lightweight Design Center. In addition, Audi organizes a VIP Car Service in the luxurious Audi A8 and Q7 TDi. Main Sponsor Swarovski Crystal Palace premiers an immersive installation that explores the relationship between crystal, light, nature, and architecture from London-based designer Asif Khan. Exclusive Champagne Sponsor Perrier-Jouët makes their Miami debut with a salon inspired by the maison's Art Nouveau history designed by Glithero's Sarah van Gameren and Tim Simpson. For the next edition of the ongoing Design Performance program at Design Miami/, Fendi invites Belgian designer Maarten De Ceulaer to develop a project that responds to Fendi's visual identity and the brand's legacy of the Modernist-inspired Pequin pattern. Design Miami's Collectors Lounge, hosted by Regalia and designed by Cassina, will welcome guests to a sophisticated catered environment.

Our eighth fair in Miami reveals the weight of a strengthened market. The increasing quality of gallery exhibitions alongside compelling cultural programming creates a sense of maturity and excitement for the rich offerings in the field of collectible design. We hope you enjoy Design Miami/ 2012!

Design Galleries

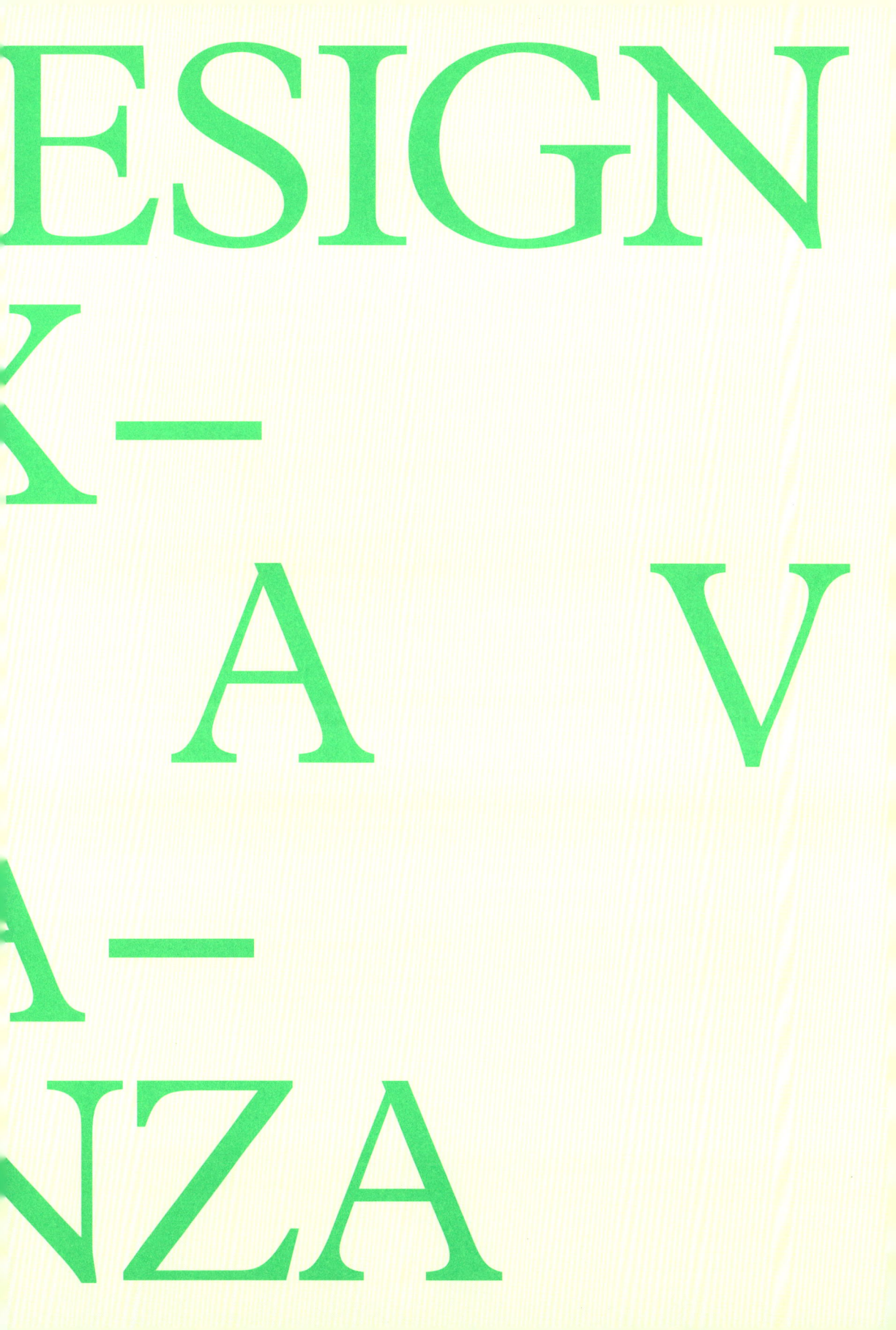

Caroline Van Hoek/
Brussels

Giampaolo Babetto
Gijs Bakker
Ralph Bakker
Alexander Blank
Helen Britton
Beatrice Brovia
Klaus Burgel
Nicolas Cheng
Willemijn De Greef
David Huycke
Beate Klockmann
Daniel Kruger
Fritz Maierhofer
Barbara Paganin
Seth Papac
Renzo Pasquale
Ruudt Peters
Robert Smit
StudyOPortable
Lisa Walker
Annamaria Zanella

Caroline van Hoek brings an overview of important and rare jewelry pieces by Gijs Bakker of the Netherlands from the1960s to now, with special thanks to Mrs. Helen Drutt for her achievements in the development of the work from Gijs Bakker in private collections and museums in the United States. Featured is silverwork by David Huycke, ceramics by Daniel Kruger and Willemijn de Greef and work by StudyOPortable, in addition to select jewelry.

The gallery opened in 2007 with a specialty in contemporary art jewelry, silver and related objects by international artists. The gallery exhibits the creative potential of the artist in its entirety through unique and specially-commissioned pieces made within the largest interpretation of the word "jewelry."

Contact/ Caroline Van Hoek
Address/ Rue Van Eyck 57, Brussels, 1050, Belgium
Call/ +32475753102
Email/ info@carolinevanhoek.be
www.carolinevanhoek.be

Marcos GT 1996
Designer/ Gijs Bakker
Year/ 2001
Materials/ Silver, amethyst, color photo and plexiglass
Dimensions/ 48 × 83 × 26 mm
Courtesy of Gijs Bakker

Carpenters Workshop Gallery/
London & Paris

Sebastian Brajkovic
Vincent Dubourg
Lonneke Gordijn &
Ralph Nauta
Mathieu Lehanneur
Frederik Molenschot
Nendo
Pablo Reinoso
Robert Stadler
Studio Job

Carpenters Workshop Gallery, with spaces in both Paris and London, is the go-to destination for exclusive, limited-edition, contemporary design-art. Straddling the border between form and function since its inception, CWG's international presence promotes an exciting lineup of established design masters alongside emerging talent.

With a full program of gallery shows and nine international art fairs this year alone, Carpenters Workshop Gallery provides an unrivaled platform for its artists to showcase their unique and limited-edition artwork to the industry and the wider public interest.

The gallery has cultivated strong relationships with the artists with which it works. Alongside those featured at Design Miami/ they also present work by Atelier Van Lieshout, Andrea Branzi, Humberto & Fernando Campana, Wendell Castle, Ingrid Donat, Johanna Grawunder, Random International and Charles Trevelyan.

Contact/ Aurelie Julien
Address/ 54, rue de la Verrerie, Paris, 75004, France
Call/ +33142788092
Email/ aurelie@carpentersworkshopgallery.com
www.carpentersworkshopgallery.com

Armoire Chinoise
Designer/ Vincent Dubourg
Year/ 2012
Materials/ Aluminum
Dimensions/ 123.5 × 52 × 224 cm
Courtesy of Carpenters Workshop Gallery

Cristina Grajales Gallery/
New York

Gael Appler
Sam Baron
Pedro Barrail
Christophe Côme
Michele Oka Doner
Sebastian Errazuriz
Jorge Lizarazo for Hechizoo
John Paul Philippe
Suzanne Tick

Since its inception in 2001, Cristina Grajales Gallery has established itself as one of the forerunners in the design world. The gallery specializes in contemporary design, while also dealing in masterpieces of the twentieth century.

Cristina Grajales Gallery focuses on cultivating the work of emerging contemporary designers. The artists represented by Cristina Grajales Gallery work in a variety of areas within the larger field of design: furniture and lighting, as well as ceramic, metal and textile design. Their work constantly pushes, blurs and in some cases erases the line between art and design.

With twenty years of experience, Grajales has established herself as a tastemaker and trendsetter both in contemporary and twentieth century design. Founded in 2001, her lecture series titled Dialogues with Design Legends at the 92nd street Y was the first of its kind. Grajales, widely considered an expert within the design field, is a frequent guest lecturer, panelist and contributor to various publications.

Cristina Grajales Gallery maintains a full program of exhibitions.
The gallery also offers advisory and design consultancy services to assist in building and maintaining important collections.

Contact/ Cristina Grajales
Address/ 10 Greene Street, 4th Floor,
New York NY, 10013 USA
Call/ +12122199941
Email/ cristina@cristinagrajalesinc.com
www.cristinagrajalesinc.com

Walking Bench
Designer/ Pedro Barrail
Year/ 2012
Materials/ Hammered metal
Dimensions/ 120 × 45 × 45 cm
Courtesy of Cristina Grajales Gallery

Demisch Danant/
New York

Pierre Guariche

Demisch Danant specializes in twentieth-century European design with an emphasis on the late 1950s through the 1980s. The gallery features the work of Maria Pergay, Pierre Paulin, Joseph Andre Motte, Pierre Guariche, Philippon & Lecoq, Rene Jean Caillette and Pentagon. The gallery also engages in a series of exhibitions concerning the intersection among architecture, design and art, including the work of Felice Varini and Krijn de Koning.

For Design Miami/ 2012, Demisch Danant will present the first show focused entirely on the works of French designer Pierre Guariche (1926 -1995). Displayed in two sections, this exhibition will present rare and significant works of 1950-1955 and 1958-1962, to highlight two distinct periods of the designer's illustrious career.

Pierre Guariche was a designer and architect working in France in the 1950s and 60s and emerged as part of a younger generation of designers interested in exploring the potential of industrial production. Guariche produced a prolific amount of furniture and lighting in conjunction with his architectural designs, in an effort to craft a total living environment based on a distinctively modern aesthetic. He is widely renowned for his commissions of the 1950s, including a collection of lighting designed for Disderot, and for the iconic "Tonneau Chair" designed for Steiner in 1954.

Contact/ Suzanne Demisch / Stephane Danant
Address/ 542 West 22nd Street, New York NY, 10011 USA
Call/ +12129895750
Email/ info@demischdanant.com
www.demischdanant.com

Armchair
Designer/ Pierre Guariche
Year/ 1953
Materials/ Ash, black enameled metal and upholstery
Dimensions/ 72 × 78 × 75 cm
Courtesy of Demisch Danant

Didier Ltd/
London

Janine Antoni
Parvine Curie
Sonya Delaunay
Claire Falkenstein
Guitou Knoop
Yayoi Kusama
Claude Lalanne
Federica Matta
Louise Nevelson
Meret Oppenheim
Alicia Penalba
Amalia del Ponte
Kiki Smith
Niki de St Phalle
Marie Vassilieff

Didier Ltd is a London-based gallery run by Didier Haspeslagh and Martine Newby Haspeslagh that specializes in jewelry by leading Modern Masters, painters and sculptors who are recognized internationally for their art. These jewels are historical pieces, produced primarily from 1940 to 1990, and blur the boundaries between art and design, while also being small, intimate expressions of their creator's art.

For Design Miami/ 2012, the gallery will be concentrating on the work of female artists, *The Sculptress Adorns - Jewellery by Women Artists*, and the accompanying catalogue will be published at the show.

The jewels themselves were made either as unique pieces, often as personal gifts for family and friends, or produced in small limited editions. Although they represent miniature works of art or wearable sculptures for the artist, they can be very large and make a dramatic statement when worn. The pieces can contain strong feminist messages as in the work by Louise Nevelson, Louise Bourgeois or Janine Antoni, while others are more delicate and feminine as seen in the jewels by Claude Lalanne or exuberant bursting with life and color as with those by Niki de St Phalle and Federica Matta.

The materials used to craft these pieces ranges from wood or brass to silver and gold, a wider selection than those used by male artists, and the use of "objets trouve" was more eclectic.

These artists' jewels will be exhibited alongside the best creations produced by twentieth century designers and architects, all of which display innovative approaches to jewelry design.

Contact/ Didier and Martine Haspeslagh
Address/ 66b Kensington Church Street, London, W8 4BY, GB
Call/ +447973800415
Email/ info@didierltd.com
www.didierltd.com

Black painted wood and gold necklace
Designer/ Louise Nevelson
Year/ Late 1960s
Materials/ Wood and gold
Dimensions/ 44 × 6.5 cm
Courtesy of Didier Ltd

Gabrielle Ammann // Gallery/ Cologne

Ron Arad
Florian Borkenhagen
Zaha Hadid
Nucleo
Satyendra Pakhalé
Rolf Sachs

One of the foremost contemporary design galleries in Europe, gabrielle ammann // gallery presents its exceptional program for the first time ever in the United States at Design Miami/ 2012.

With over twenty years of experience curating exhibitions and initiating projects, Gabrielle Ammann has collaborated with the most significant figures in architecture and design including Ron Arad, Marc Newson and Zaha Hadid. In 2006, she established a permanent gallery space to create a forum to explore the intersections among architecture, fine art and design. The gallery exhibits iconic works by important designers while cultivating the best emerging designers.

For its inaugural presentation at Design Miami/, the gallery is displaying highlights from the collection including a rare Ron Arad chaise longue and the 'Eolia' stools by Zaha Hadid, originally designed for Louis Vuitton. In conversation with these works is the captivating 'Resin Fossil Table' by Studio Nucleo as well as the sculptural 'White Swan' by Indian designer Satyendra Pakhalé, both debuting at Design Miami/.

Addressing the individual needs of clients, gabrielle ammann // gallery offers a range of services including acquisitions, collection management and curatorial work. With extensive interior design experience, Gabrielle Ammann provides consultation for both private and public spaces, creating sophisticated environments by ingeniously integrating art and design. Working directly with important artists and designers, the gallery presents the opportunity to commission unique works of art and design for collections.

Contact/ Gabrielle Ammann
Address/ Teutoburger Strasse 27, Cologne, 50678, Germany
Call/ +492219328803
Email/ contact@ammann-gallery.com
www.ammann-gallery.com

Resin Fossil Table 02
Designer/ Nucleo
Year/ 2012
Materials/ Epoxy resin
Dimensions/ 280 × 120 × 75 cm
Courtesy of gabrielle ammann // gallery

Galerie BSL/
Paris

David Adjaye
Taher Chemirik
Noé Duchaufour-Lawrance
Charles Kalpakian

Established in Paris, Galerie BSL commissions unique and limited-edition pieces that explore the shifting borders between art and design, sculpture and function, emotions created by the human hand and those born from technological innovation, modeling new frontiers in the approach to the object. The gallery represents both established names and emerging talent working in today's international Design Art scene.

In Miami, Galerie BSL unveils the first pieces of furniture by Taher Chemirik, the internationally renowned jewelry designer named by Time as one of today's most influential designers, and whose creations are featured in the Musée des Arts Décoratifs in Paris. Brass, copper and sardonyx hard stone give shape to beautifully sculpted pieces: a five meter long chandelier trails a copper and brass flower train; a three meter long sea of brass waves stands as a screen. Along with his coffee tables, these sensual, refined and dramatic "Interior Treasures" vouch for the wealth of a talent that expresses itself through volume, whatever the scale.

Unveiled last June in Basel, the 'Naturoscopie' collection by Noé Duchaufour-Lawrance is represented by the black lighting and new white versions. Design Art is here infused with an emotional imprint, one of nature when the sunlight filters through the foliage of a tree via LEDs, and digital programming.

On the walls, the eye-catching cabinets by French-Lebanese Charles Kalpakian are true functional paintings flirting with the spirit of Vasarely. David Adjaye's copper mirror and three vessel 'Star' collection for Gaia & Gino offer another play on geometry. These micro-architectures in copper and black Swarovski crystals are presented for the first time in the US by 'Designer of the Year 2011', one of the world's leading architects of his generation.

Contact/ Béatrice Saint-Laurent
Address/ 23, rue Charlot, Paris, 75003, France
Call/ +33144789414
Email/ bsaintlaurent@galeriebsl.com
www.galeriebsl.com

'Rough Sea' screen
Designer/ Taher Chemirik
Year/ 2012
Materials/ Brass
Dimensions/ 300 × 50 × 230 cm
Courtesy of Alain Cornu

Galerie DOWNTOWN – François Laffanour/ Paris

Ron Arad
Le Corbusier
Choi Byung Hoon
Pierre Jeanneret
François-Xavier Lalanne
Serge Mouille
George Nakashima
Jean Prouvé
Charlotte Perriand
Jean Royère
Ettore Sottsass

When François Laffanour opened Galerie Downtown on the rue de Seine in 1982, he showed the work of Jean Royère, Mathieu Matégot, Charles and Ray Eames and George Nelson. He swiftly realized that the work of Le Corbusier, Jean Prouvé, Charlotte Perriand and Pierre Jeanneret also had to be recognized along with an in-depth examination of their careers.

These fascinating figures thought and created as architects, designers, craftspeople and industrial manufacturers. At one time overlooked, their rediscovery is largely due to the patient but unflagging work of Laffanour, whose reputation has henceforth been associated with architects' furniture.

He managed to acquire the archives of the Steph Simon Gallery, which produced and sold the works of Jean Prouvé and Charlotte Perriand between 1956 and 1974, and was an invaluable source of information. Just like the Steph Simon Gallery, Galerie Downtown exhibited Serge Mouille's lights and Georges Jouve's ceramics, which provide a powerful accompaniment to furniture.

Keen to spread the word about creative figures he admires, Laffanour was the first person in France to show Charles and Ray Eames, Mathieu Matégot, George Nakashima, George Nelson, Isamu Nogushi, Jean Prouvé, Charlotte Perriand and Jean Royère.

A gesture, a thought, a creative sensibility, a certain poetry, a spirit of their time - all help to explain the choices made by Laffanour with regard to the works of Ettore Sottsass, George Nakashima, Takis and Choï, along with architect and designer Ron Arad, who has been represented by the gallery since 1994.

Contact/ François Laffanour
Address/ 18 & 33 rue de Seine, Paris, 75006, France
Call/ +33146338241
Email/ contact@galeriedowntown.com
www.galeriedowntown.com

Bookshelves
Designer/ Charlotte Perriand
Year/ 1958
Materials/ Folded steel, wood and formica
Dimensions/ 140 × 184 × 46 cm
Courtesy of Marie Clérin

Galerie Jacques Lacoste/
Paris

Georges Jouve
Alexandre Noll
Jean Royère

Specializing in twentieth-century decorative arts, Jacques Lacoste has set out to promote French design of the 1950s.

Jacques Lacoste began by taking a booth at the Serpette flea market in Saint Ouen in 1986. He opened his first gallery in the carré Rive Gauche in 1997 and moved to the Rue de Seine in Saint-Germain des Prés in February 2008.

Particularly sensitive to the work and the universe of Jean Royère, Jacques Lacoste acquired the designer's archives in 1997 and dedicated two exhibitions to him in his Parisian gallery in 1999 and 2003 and in New York at the Sonnabend Gallery in collaboration with Galerie Patrick Seguin in 2008. In 2003 he brought his expertise to bear on the publication of a book on Royère, 'Jean Royère,' by Pierre-Emmanuel Martin-Vivier, Editions Norma, Paris, and is now working on his catalogue raisonné.

Very passionate about 1950s decorative arts, Jacques Lacoste exhibits lighting by Serge Mouille, sculptures by Alexandre Noll and ceramics by Georges Jouve, Elisabeth Joulia, Pierre Szekely, Valentine Schlegel and André Borderie.

In February 2008, Lacoste opened a new gallery at 12 Rue de Seine with an exhibition of works by French sculptor Alexandre Noll. In September 2009 the gallery organized the first retrospective exhibition on the glassmaker and designer Max Ingrand and contributed to the publication of his monograph 'Max Ingrand: du verre à la lumière' by Pierre-Emmanuel Martin-Vivier (editions Norma, September 2009).

Contact/ Jacques Lacoste
Address/ 12 rue de Seine, Paris, 75006, France
Call/ +33140204182
Email/ lacoste.jacques@wanadoo.fr

Set of Four Egg Chairs
Designer/ Jean Royère
Year/ 1952
Materials/ Ashtree, velvet and mohair velvet
Dimensions/ 54 × 46 × 82 cm
Courtesy of Hervé Lewandowski

Galerie kreo/
Paris

Pierre Charpin
Gino Sarfatti
Wieki Somers

At Galerie kreo, Clémence and Didier Krzentowski present exclusive limited-edition pieces by Ronan & Erwan Bouroullec, Pierre Charpin, Naoto Fukasawa, Konstantin Grcic, Hella Jongerius, Jasper Morrison, Marc Newson, Maarten Van Severen and Martin Szekely, as well as work by François Bauchet, Humberto & Fernando Campana, Alessandro Mendini, Jerszy Seymour, Studio Wieki Somers and others.

Works by these designers are part of the permanent collections of the most important private collections and museums around the world. Galerie kreo is currently preparing the catalogues raisonnés of the work of Ronan & Erwan Bouroullec, Marc Newson and Martin Szekely.

Parallel to championing contemporary design, Galerie kreo also offers rare and exceptional vintage lamps with a focus on the Italian avant-garde. The Krzentowskis started their collection of lights 30 years ago, acquiring works ranging from the 1950s until today.

Didier Krzentowski is a licensed expert in design and contemporary art and is a member of the Union Française des Experts and Assesseur de la Commission de Conciliation et d'Expertise Douanière.

Contact/ Clémence and Didier Krzentowski
Address/ 31 rue Dauphine, Paris, 75006, France
Call/ +33153102300
Email/ info@galeriekreo.com
www.galeriekreo.com

Crescendo
Designer/ Pierre Charpin
Year/ 2012
Materials/ Bisazza tiles
Dimensions/ 155 × 60 × 35 cm
Courtesy of Galerie kreo

Galerie Maria Wettergren/
Paris

Keiji Ashizawa
Mathias Bengtsson
Louise Campbell
Erling Christoffersen
GamFratesi
Rasmus Fenhann
Ditte Hammerstroem
Astrid Krogh
Mikko Paakkanen
Hans Sandgren Jakobsen
Grethe Soerensen
Ilkka Suppanen
Eske Rex
Tora Urup

Galerie Maria Wettergren specializes in twenty-first century Scandinavian design of limited-edition furniture, lighting and art objects. The main interest of the gallery is the experimental design born of our present time, which opens up future perspectives while keeping in mind the experience of the past. New ideas, technologies and materials are combined with the Scandinavian tradition of excellent craftsmanship, giving rise to sculptural and poetic design objects with multiple purposes. The gallery is promoting both established designers and emerging talents from the new Nordic design scene through gallery editions, exhibitions and fairs.

The gallery exhibits and produces pieces by pioneering Scandinavian designers from the past twenty years such as Mathias Bengtsson, Astrid Krogh, Ditte Hammerstroem, Cecilie Manz, Niels Hvass, Rasmus Fenhann, Erling Christoffersen, Line Depping, Jakob Joergensen, Hans Sandgren Jakobsen, Harri Koskinen, Ilkka Suppanen, Timo Salli, Mikko Paakkanen, GamFratesi and Tora Urup.

Contact/ Maria Wettergren
Address/ 18 rue Guénégaud, Paris, 75006, FR
Call/ +33677632881
Email/ info@mariawettergren.com
www.mariawettergren.com

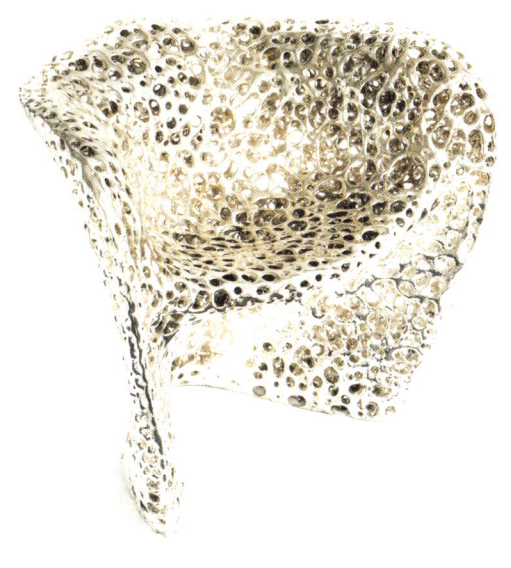

Cellular Chair
Year/2011
Designer/ Mathias Bengtsson
Materials/ Silver on resin
Dimensions/ 82 × 64 × 74 cm
Courtesy of Martin Scott-Jupp

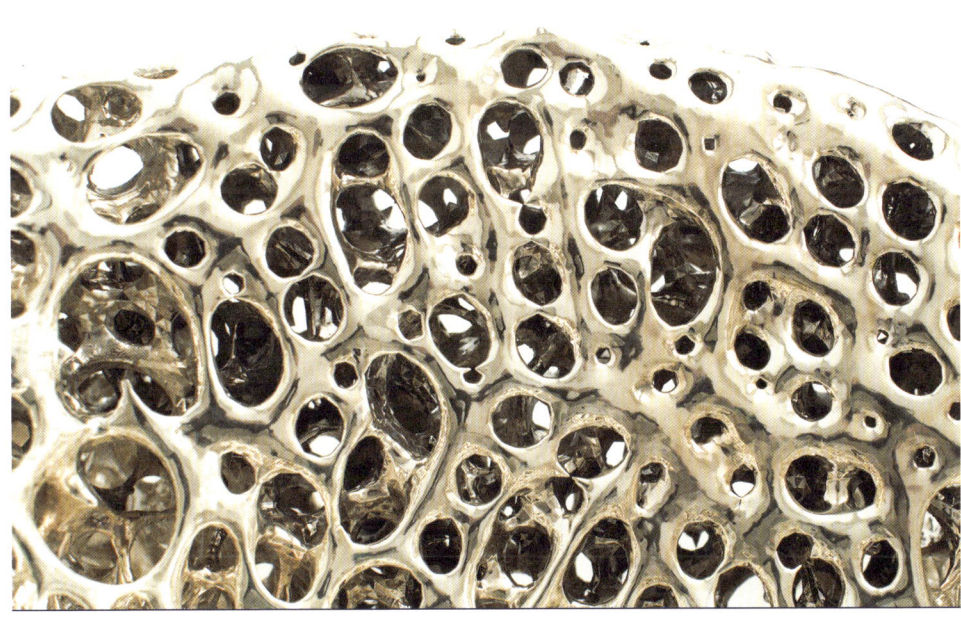

Galerie Patrick Seguin/
Paris

Le Corbusier
Pierre Jeanneret
Charlotte Perriand
Jean Prouvé
Jean Royère

Established in 1989 in Paris in a three hundred square meter space (gallery and offices designed by Ateliers Jean Nouvel in 2003), the gallery showcases the talent of French designers from the 1950s such as Jean Prouvé, Charlotte Perriand, Le Corbusier, Pierre Jeanneret and Jean Royère. Today, these designers are recognized as major contributors to the history of design in the twentieth century.

Patrick Seguin's impeccable eye for amazing artworks made it possible to present unseen exhibitions in international renowned galleries and his reputation based on seriousness and professionalism enabled him to collaborate with some of the most prestigious museums worldwide.

For its eighth participation in Design Miami/, Galerie Patrick Seguin is presenting furniture that Le Corbusier and Pierre Jeanneret created for the paramount urban-planning and architectural project for the city of Chandigarh in India. Highlights include conference tables, armchairs and sofa, floor lamps, day bed and wood and wicker lounge chairs.

Contact/ Gwenaelle Lannuzel
Address/ 5 rue des Taillandiers, Paris, 75011, France
Call/ +33147003235
Email/ info@patrickseguin.com
www.patrickseguin.com

Chandigarh
Designer/ Pierre Jeanneret
Year/ 1956–59
Materials/ Wood
Dimensions/ Variable
Courtesy of Galerie Patrick Seguin

Galerie VIVID/
Rotterdam

Studio Glithero
Gerrit Th. Rietveld
Richard Woods /
Sebastian Wrong

Founded by Saskia Copper and Aad Krol in 1999, Galerie VIVID was among the first to show contemporary design in the context of both design and art.

For Design Miami/ 2012, Galerie VIVID is proud to present new contemporary designs alongside several iconic pieces by Gerrit Rietveld, the great Dutch furniture designer and architect.

A highlight of the exhibition will be an unused Rietveld Red Blue chair, executed by Gerard A. van Groenekan. This chair was ordered by an American architect in 1965 but never made it to America and was put in storage. Fifty years later, the chair along with the original shipping crate will be on display.

Galerie VIVID will also debut an edition of four Bent Wood Tables by British designer Richard Woods and Sebastian Wrong. The colorful hand-painted low tables form together an installation that crosses boundaries between design and art.

Contact/ Saskia Copper / Aad Krol
Address/ Red Apple Building, Scheepmakershaven 17
Rotterdam, 3011VA, Netherlands
Call/ +31104136321
Email/ info@galerievivid.com
www.galerievivid.com

Unused Red Blue chair with original shipping crate
Designer/ Gerrit Th. Rietveld
Year/ 1965
Materials/ Painted wood
Dimensions/ 80 × 66 × 87 cm / 100 × 87 × 66 cm
Courtesy of Galerie VIVID

Bent Wood Tables
Designer/ Richard Woods / Sebastian Wrong
Year/ 2012
Materials/ Hand painted birch wood and colored glass
Dimensions/ 73 × 73 × 54 cm / 51 × 51 × 65 cm
Courtesy of Galerie VIVID

Galleria Rossella Colombari/ Milan

Architetti Asnago and Vender
B.B.P.R.
Osvaldo Borsani
Andrea Branzi
Sergio Cappelli/ Patrizia Ranzo
Joe Colombo
Angelo Mangiarotti
Carlo Mollino
Roberto Monsani
Gino Levi Montalcini
Ico Parisi
Giò Ponti
Ettore Sottsass
Carlo Zen

Rossella Colombari was born in Turin to a family of prestigious antique dealers. In 1980, she founded Galleria Colombari in Milan and focused her attention on the discovery and research of works by the Italian architect Carlo Mollino.

For more than three decades, Galleria Colombari has dealt with pieces from the most important Italian designers of the twentieth century, such as Giò Ponti, Carlo Mollino, Carlo Graffi, Ico Parisi, Franco Albini, Osvaldo Borsani, Guglielmo Ulrich, Andrea Branzi, Ettore Sottsass and Alessandro Mendini. The gallery has actively promoted their work in national and international markets.

The gallery has more recently begun to expand its horizon by dealing in works by American designers from the 1960s and 1970s, such as Paul Evans, Philip & Kelvin Laverne and Phillip Lloyd Powell.

Contact/ Rossella Colombari
Address/ Via Maroncelli 10, Milan, 20154, Italy
Call/ +393338084476
Email/ galleria.colombari@galleriacolombari.com
www.galleriacolombari.com

Desk
Designer/ Giò Ponti
Year/ 1955
Materials/ Metal structure and plastic laminate top with a brushed brass border.
Dimensions/ 169.5 × 80 × 76.5 cm
Courtesy of Galleria Rossella Colombari

Gallery SEOMI/
Seoul

Byunghoon Choi
Se Hwa Bae
Jong Sun Bahk
Jin Jang
Myung Sun Kang
Sanghoon Kim
Hun Chung Lee

Bringing contemporary design movements within one frame, Gallery SEOMI introduces works that reflect the new constructionism and organicism of Korea. These works show a refined and eclectic vision and have become modern classics within their own culture.

The works include those of Korean designers Bahk Jongsun, Bae Sehwa, Jang Jin, Kang Myungsun, Kim Sanghoon, Choi Byunghoon and Lee Hunchung, and are devoted to the idea of craftsmanship and to maintaining an originality that goes beyond contemporary ideas of form and style. They present dynamic yet understated design objects that represent the essence of modern life.

To enhance the aesthetic of modern Asian organicism with a considered approach to function, the recent versions of works, meticulously hand-made, possess their own context and reveal a unique design. They become iconic works and reflect modern ideas toward the principle and philosophy of craftsmanship and architectural naturalism. Beyond beauty, they are focused on new forms of structure and utility that rediscover the diverse style of living culture. As showcasing the interaction within the realms of design, art and architecture, they suggest new ideas and perspectives of the culture within integrated boundaries.

Contact/ Lia Moon
Address/ Chungdamdong 97-19, Gangnam, Seoul, 135-100, Korea
Call/ +8225117980
Email/ lia@seomituus.com
www.galleryseomi.com

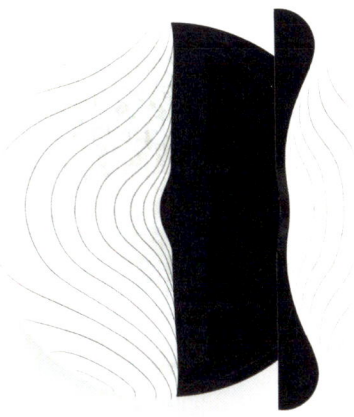

From the Glitter
Designer/ Myung Sun Kang
Year/ 2012
Materials/ Mother-of-pearl on wood and
lacquered in black
Dimensions/ 59 × 24 cm
Courtesy of Gallery SEOMI

Bada planters
Designer/ Hun Chung Lee
Year/ 2012
Materials/ Glazed ceramic in traditional
grayish-blue powdered celadon
Dimensions/ Various
Courtesy of Gallery SEOMI

Hostler Burrows/
New York

Berndt Friberg
Henry Heerup
Axel Einar Hjorth
Finn Juhl
Birger Kaipiainen
Wilhelm Kåge
Bruno Mathsson
Axel Salto

Kim Hostler and Juliet Burrows founded their New York gallery Antik in 1998 and have consistently led the evolving market of Nordic design, championing and promoting the work of Scandinavia's most prominent designers of the twentieth century. The gallery focuses on exceptional and unique examples of studio ceramics, cabinetmaker furniture and hand woven textiles by the master artisans and architects of the period.

After fourteen years in its TribeCa home, the gallery, which now bears the owners' names – Hostler Burrows – has opened at its new location of 51 East 10th St., in the heart of one of New York City's richest destinations for design and decorative arts.

For Design Miami/ 2012 the gallery features ceramic works by Axel Salto, Wilhelm Kåge and Birger Kaipianen, and selected furniture from the "Sandhamn" suite by the Swedish architect Axel Einar Hjorth.

Contact/ Kim Hostler
Address/ 51 East 10th Street, New York NY, 10003, USA
Call/ +12123430471
Email/ info@hostlerburrows.com
www.hostlerburrows.com

Grouping of vases
Designer/ Berndt Friberg
Year/ 1934–1965
Materials/ Porcelain
Dimensions/ 15–36 cm
Courtesy of Hostler Burrows

Industry Gallery/ Washington DC & Los Angeles

Maarten De Ceulaer
Jens Praet

Industry Gallery, the only US gallery focused exclusively on twenty-first century design, opened in January 2010 in Washington D.C. Occupying over 4000 square feet of space in a converted auto-repair shop, the gallery holds temporary exhibitions of work by designers selected for their ability to illuminate a broad spectrum of international design.

As the gallery's name suggests, Industry presents designers who are creating new and innovative works with the use of modern industrial materials. These materials range from common items such as recycled magazine paper and glass to more sophisticated materials such as aluminum and carbon fiber.

The gallery's generous exhibition area allows each designer to tell his or her own story through site-specific installations designed to transform the perception of space. By loading the interior of the gallery with disparate items, each designer evokes complex and multiple associations to create a three-dimensional painting.

The gallery opened its second exhibition space in Los Angeles in March 2011, in the historic Pacific Design Center, one of the West Coast's top design destinations and home to a branch of the Museum of Contemporary Art (MOCA).

Contact/ Craig Appelbaum
Address/ 1358 Florida Avenue, NE, Suite 200
Washington DC, 20002, USA
Call/ +12023991730
Email/ craig@industrygallerydc.com
www.industrygallerydc.com

Side Table
Designer/ Jens Praet
Year/ 2011
Materials/ Shredded documents and binding agent
Dimensions/ 40 × 85 × 75 cm
Courtesy of Industry Gallery

Mutation Lounge
Designer/ Maarten de Ceulaer
Year/ 2012
Materials/ Foam spheres and durable rubber
Dimensions/ 85 × 60 × 60 cm
Courtesy of Industry Gallery

Jason Jacques Inc./
New York

Thorvald Bindesbol
Rene Buthaud
Jean Carries
Paul Dachsel
Albert-Louis Dammouse
Theodore Deck
Auguste Delaherche
Lucien Levy-Dhurmer
Morten Lobner Espersen
Mason Gareth
Michael Geertsen
Hector Guimard
Edmond Lachenal
Max Laueger
Axel Salto

Jason Jacques Gallery of New York holds the world's finest and most comprehensive collection of 1870-1920 European Art Pottery. Specializing in the Art Pottery Renaissance centered in 1890's France, the collection includes Art Nouveau and Japoniste masterworks by stoneware artists Ernest Chaplet, Jean Carries, Edmond Lachenal and Adrien Dalpayrat, in addition to the vast holdings of iridescent lusterware artists Lucien Lévy-Dhurmer, Clément Massier, and Vilmos Zsolnay.

In addition to its comprehensive collection of nineteenth century European Art Pottery, the gallery also represents innovative contemporary ceramic artists including Michael Geertsen, Mason Gareth, and Morten Lobner Espersen.

Contact/ Jason Jacques
Address/ 29 East 73rd Street #1,
New York NY, 10021, USA
Call/ +12125357500
Email/ info@jasonjacques.com
www.jasonjacques.com

Gothic Vase
Designer/ Geogre Hoentschel
Year/ ca. 1890
Materials/ Stoneware
Dimensions/ 19.5 cm
Courtesy of Jason Jacques Inc

Modern Ornament Vase
Designer/ Christopher Dresser
Year/ ca. 1867
Materials/ Porcelain
Dimensions/ 51 × 24 cm
Courtesy of Jason Jacques Inc.

Johnson Trading Gallery/
Queens

Kwangho Lee
Robert Loughlin

Johnson Trading Gallery is a leading international furniture gallery established in 2001 as a forum to produce and exhibit significant contemporary design projects and vintage twentieth century pieces. The gallery fosters collaborative efforts with emerging architects, designers and artists who push the boundaries of traditional furniture making.

Johnson Trading Gallery has shown at Design Miami/ since 2007 and recently relocated from Manhattan to Queens.

Contact/ Paul Johnson
Address/ 4742 43rd Street, Queens NY, 11377, USA
Call/ +12129251110
Email/ info@johnsontradinggallery.com
www.johnsontradinggallery.com

Untitled
Designer/ Robert Loughlin
Year/ 2007
Materials/ Paint on found cabinet
Dimensions/ 79 × 43 × 77.5 cm
Courtesy of Johnson Trading Gallery

Jousse Entreprise/
Paris

Emmanuel Boos
André Borderie
Michel Boyer
Le Corbusier
Pierre Jeanneret
Georges Jouve
Mathieu Matégot
Kristin McKirdy
Serge Mouille
Rick Owens
Pierre Paulin
Maria Pergay
Charlotte Perriand
Jean Prouvé
Jean Royère
Roger Tallon

For more than thirty years, Philippe Jousse has contributed to the growing recognition of designers such as Jean Prouvé, Charlotte Perriand, Le Corbusier, Pierre Jeanneret, Georges Jouve, Mathieu Matégot, André Borderie, Alexandre Noll, Serge Mouille and Jean Royére - all innovators of design in their time.

Jousse Entreprise comprises two galleries: one located at 18 rue de Seine in the 6th arrondissement of Paris dedicated to furniture from the 1950s and also from the 1970s; the space at 6 rue Saint-Claude is dedicated to contemporary art.

Contact/ Philippe Jousse
Address/ 18 rue de Seine, Paris, 75006, France
Call/ +33153821360
Email/ infos@jousse-entreprise.com
www.jousse-entreprise.com

Double cabinet
Designer/ Jean Prouvé
Year/ ca.1950
Materials/ Wood, bent steel and aluminum
Dimensions/ 210 × 186.5 × 46 cm
Courtesy of Adrien Dirand

Magen H Gallery/
New York

Pierre Chapo
Georges Jouve
Ceramics by La Borne
Charlotte Perriand
Jean Prouvé
Jean Royère

Since 1997, Magen H Gallery has exhibited significant design in sculpture, decorative arts, architecture and ceramics, with a special emphasis given to French post-war design. Establishing greater visibility and appreciation for important works previously limited in reception, the curated collection emphasizes craft and concept exempt from ephemeral trends. Synthesizing modern and mid-century designers, the gallery exhibits works that transcend form and function.

Magen H Gallery is pleased to announce the book release of La Borne: 1940-1980, produced by gallery founder Hugues Magen, specialist and collector in French post-war design and decorative arts.

Contact/ Hugues Magen / Nathalie Dheedene
Address/ 54 East 11th Street, New York NY, 10003, USA
Call/ +12127778670
Email/ gallery@magenxxcentury.com
www.magenxxcentury.com

Large Vase
Designer/ Jean and Jacqueline Lerat
Year/ ca. 1969
Materials/ Ceramic
Dimensions/ 38.1 × 14 × 78.7 cm
Courtesy of Magen H Gallery

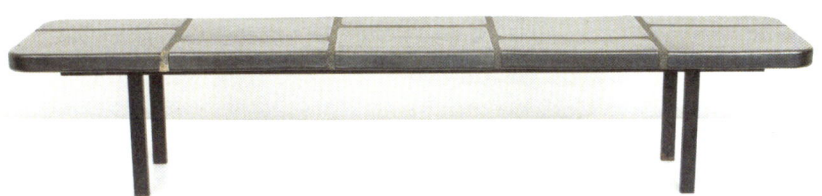

Coffee Table
Designer/ Georges Jouve
Year/ ca. 1955
Materials/ Black glazed ceramic tiles and painted metal base
Dimensions/ 194.1 × 34.5 × 39.4 cm
Courtesy of Magen H Gallery

Mark McDonald/
Hudson

Alexander Calder
Charles and Ray Eames
Claire Falkenstein
Maija Grotell
Max Ingram
Art Smith

Located in Hudson, New York, Mark McDonald Gallery is the latest exhibition space for Mark McDonald, a preeminent dealer in mid-twentieth century decorative arts, including furniture designed by architects such as Frank Lloyd Wright, Gerrit Rietveld, Alvar Aalto and Frank Gehry.

McDonald's expertise in the field is the result of three decades of experience, organizing landmark exhibitions on Frank Lloyd Wright, Charles and Ray Eames, Art Smith and the Studio Jewelry Movement, Nordic Design, American Studio Ceramics and the Abstract Expressionists. He began in New York City in 1982 at his ground-breaking Fifty/50 Gallery in Greenwich Village. In 1995 he moved to Manhattan's Meatpacking District on Gansevoort Street. And in 2002, McDonald embarked on a new venture, moving north to the Hudson Valley.

McDonald's current gallery is housed in a preserved three-story building that was originally constructed as a department store in 1910. The first floor houses furniture, textiles, books, ceramics and lighting and features jewelry by Alexander Calder, Harry Bertoia, Margaret De Patta, Art Smith and Claire Falkenstein. The second floor is used for gallery exhibitions and the third houses offices and a research library.

McDonald and the gallery are perhaps best known for advising important collectors and museums such as: Vitra Design Museum, Los Angeles County Museum of Art, Montreal Museum of Decorative Arts, The Daphne Farago Jewelry Collection (recently given to the Museum of Fine Arts, Boston), the John Waddell "American Modern" exhibition at The Metropolitan Museum of Art and the Art Smith "Village to Vogue" exhibit at The Brooklyn Museum.

Contact/ Mark McDonald
Address/ 555 Warren Street, Hudson NY, 12534, USA
Call/ +15188289282
Email/ 330@markmcdonald.biz
www.markmcdonald.biz

Eames Storage Units
Year/ 1951–1954
Designer/ Charles and Ray Eames
Materials/ Birch plywood, laquered masonite, laminate and zinc-plated steel
Dimensions/ Various
Courtesy of Mark McDonald

Moderne Gallery/
Philadelphia

David Ebner
Wharton Esherick
Viola Frey
Sam Maloof
Edward Moulthrop
George Nakashima
Peter Voulkos
Robert Worth

Founded in 1984 by Robert Aibel, Moderne Gallery is an internationally recognized gallery for twentieth century decorative arts, with a primary specialization in work from the American Craft and Studio Movement from 1925-1990. The gallery holds a large collection of work by Wharton Esherick, George Nakashima, Sam Maloof, Arthur Espenet Carpenter, Wendell Castle, David Ebner, Peter Voulkos, Paul Soldner, Edward Moulthrop, James Prestini and most of the major figures of the movement.

Contact/ Bob Aibel
Address/ 111 North 3rd Street, Philadelphia PA, 19106, USA
Call/ +12159238536
Email/ info@modernegallery.com
www.modernegallery.com

Rocking Chair
Designer/ Sam Maloof
Year/ 1977
Materials/ American black walnut
Dimensions/ 68 × 109 × 117 cm
Courtesy of Moderne Gallery

Pizzicato
Designer/ Wharton Esherick
Year/ 1931
Materials/ Rosewood, oak, walnut and aluminum
Dimensions/ 63.5 × 43 × 203 cm
Courtesy of Moderne Gallery

Nilufar Gallery/
Milan

Michael Anastassiades
Maarten De Ceulaer
Peder Moos
Michelangelo Pistoletto

Nilufar is one of Italy's most active galleries in the fields of historical and contemporary design and in the field of antique oriental carpets and furniture. The gallery, now housed in a three-story space on Milan's prestigious via della Spiga, was founded by Nina Yashar in 1979 and since then has presented exhibitions of unmistakable style - always eclectic, and always to be read in novel, unexpected ways.

Nilufar pursues the development of contemporary artist-designers working for the gallery while discovering new international design talents and emerging artists making their debut in Italy.

Contact/ Nina Yashar
Address/ Via della Spiga 32, Milan, 20121, Italy
Call/ +3902780193
Email/ agira@nilufar.com
www.nilufar.com

Table
Designer/ Peder Moos
Year/ 1947
Materials/ Walnut and beech wood
Dimensions/ 120 × 91 × 65 cm / 95 × 93 × 67 cm
Courtesy of Nilufar Gallery

Ornamentum/
Hudson

David Bielander
David Clarke
Johanna Dahm
Sam Tho Duong
Ute Eitzenhöfer
Jantje Fleischhut
Karl Fritsch
John Iversen
Jens Rüdiger Lorenzen
Bruno Martinazzi
Atelier Ted Noten
Gerd Rothmann
Giovanni Sicuro
Terhi Tolvanen
Petra Zimmermann

Founded in 2002, Ornamentum exhibits a dynamic collection of contemporary jewelry as well as related objects and artworks. Ornamentum hosts numerous exhibitions yearly in their gallery space – one of the world's largest – dedicated specifically to contemporary jewelry-artworks, where featured designer-artists display their work in conceptual installations.

Celebrating ten years this past summer, Ornamentum is well-established as a major force for introducing this exciting medium to new audiences, working to help build many of the world's most significant public and private collections of contemporary jewelry and playing a pivotal role in numerous acquisitions of important works by key museums.

For the occasion of Ornamentum's fifth presentation at Design Miami/, a salient collection of works will be introduced to this exclusive audience, including a Design Miami/ premiere of Swiss designer Johanna Dahm's project "William Tell's Shot"- a presentation of rings created by shooting through silver and gold bars or coins with a machine gun.

The exhibition also features a strong group of new and signature works, accompanied by a catalog created for this occasion, by German jeweler Gerd Rothmann, known for creating highly-personalized works using the imprints of the finger or other body parts, often taken from the wearer or his/her loved ones.

Contact/ Stefan Friedemann
Address/ 506 Warren Street, Hudson NY, 12534, USA
Call/ +15186716770
Email/ info@ornamentumgallery.com
www.ornamentumgallery.com

Out of the Workshop of Tiffany Brooch
Designer/ Gerd Rothmann
Year/ 2012
Materials/ Gold and zirconia
Dimensions/ 7 × 6.5 × 1.7cm
Courtesy of Felicitas Rall-Wirtz

Pierre Marie Giraud/
Brussels

Martine Bedin
Rose Cabat
Kishi Eiko
Fukumoto Fuku
Jean Girel
Valerie Hermans
Louiselio
Tony Marsh
Kristin McKirdy
Ritsue Mishima
Ron Nagle
Barbara Nanning
Magdalene Odundo
Nadia Pasquer
Sterling Ruby
Kazuo Takiguchi
Annick Tapernoux
Alev Ebbüzziya Siesbye
Akiyama Yo
Kimura Yoshiro
Kaneshige Yuho
Miyashita Zenji

Specializing in contemporary decorative arts, Pierre Marie Giraud represents international artists working with glass, ceramics and silver, and collaborates with designers for the production of unique objects and limited editions. A rich selection of modern and contemporary pieces makes the gallery's ceramics program particularly noteworthy.

Pierre Marie Giraud represents the best among European, North American and Japanese artists, and regularly features solo or thematic exhibitions of their work. The gallery issues publications about the artists featured in its exhibitions, collaborates with multiple museums on the promotion of modern and contemporary ceramics and participates frequently in international fairs.

Contact/ Pierre Marie Giraud
Address/ 7 rue de Praetere, Brussels, 1050, Belgium
Call/ +3225030351
Email/ info@pierremariegiraud.com
www.pierremariegiraud.com

Babel
Designer/ Ritsue Mishima
Year/ 2012
Materials/ Glass
Dimensions/ 59 × 36 × 32 cm
Courtesy of Pierre Marie Giraud

Priveekollektie
Contemporary Art | Design/
Heusden aan de Maas

Reinier Bosch
Nigel Coates
Dominic Harris
Richard Hutten
De Intuïtiefabriek
Arik Levy
Ifeanyi Oganwu
Rolf Sachs
Thukral & Tagra

Priveekollektie Contemporary Art | Design represents internationally-recognized artists and designers, and provides young and upcoming talents with a platform for showing their exceptional work. Key in the collection is the combination of contemporary art and limited-edition design and the crossing of the fine line between both disciplines.

Before opening the gallery in 2006, Irving and Miriam van Dijk avidly collected art and design.
Their personal approach, knowledge and taste have developed one of the leading galleries for collectible design in Europe, with exceptional exhibitions and participation in renowned international fairs.

Address/ Pelsestraat 13-15, Heusden aan de Maas, 5256AT, Netherlands
Call/ +31416858424
Email/ gallery@priveekollektie.com
www.priveekollektie.com

Ornatu
Designer/ De Intuïtiefabriek
Year/ 2012
Materials/ Walnut, powder coated steel, copper, glass, mirror and porcelain
Dimensions/ 104 × 35 × 180 cm
Courtesy of Priveekollektie Contemporary Art | Design

R 20th Century/
New York

Wendell Castle
Joaquim Tenreiro
David Wiseman

R 20th Century is a New York based gallery representing historical and contemporary design from the United States, South America, Europe and Asia.

Founded in 1997 by Zesty Meyers and Evan Snyderman, the Tribeca gallery runs an exhibition program with the goal of promoting a closer study, appreciation and preservation of twentieth and twenty-first century design.

R 20th Century specializes in unique and rare vintage works by designers including Wendell Castle, Greta Magnusson Grossman, Poul Kjærholm, Verner Panton, Sergio Rodrigues, Joaquim Tenreiro and Jose Zanine among others.

The gallery also represents contemporary designers Hugo França, Hun-Chung Lee, Renate Muller, David Wiseman and Jeff Zimmerman.

Contact/ Zesty Meyers / Evan Snyderman
Address/ 82 Franklin Street, New York NY, 10013, USA
Call/ +12123437979
Email/ zesty@r20thcentury.com
www.r20thcentury.com

Unique scultural table
Designer/ Wendell Castle
Date/ 1966
Materials/ Walnut
Dimensions/ 52.7 × 176.5 × 53.9 cm
Courtesy of Sherry Griffin for R 20th Century

Venice Projects/
Venice

Pieke Bergmans

Venice Projects provides internationally recognized contemporary artists and designers with the opportunity to express their creativity in a new medium – glass. Through its cultural planning activities and site-specific projects, Venice Projects develops educational opportunities for dialogue and experimentation in the use of glass in contemporary art. Venice Projects is the producer of an official event of the Venice Biennale dedicated to contemporary art in glass, Glasstress, which will have a new edition opening in June 2013.

Contact/ Adriano Berengo
Address/ Dorsoduro 868, Venice, 30123, Italy
Call/ + 390412413189
Email/ berengoadriano@gmail.com
www.veniceprojects.com

Making of (Venitian Love Streetlights)
Designer/ Pieke Bergmans
Year/ 2012
Materials/ Glass and iron
Dimensions/ Variable
Courtesy of Pieke Bergmans and Berengo Studio Private Collection

R

NQUIR

N   G

NDS

Antonella Villanova/ Florence

Delfina Delettrez

The show will display a careful selection of her most excellent and unique jewelry works, some representative of the collections she created between 2007 and 2012 that are rarely shown. The pieces specifically produced for Design Miami/ are presented in the frame of a conceptual installation.

Nine mirrored columns equipped with rotating iron top plates compose the setting of the work, hosting a single piece each. Magnifying glasses mounted on the columns' sides will offer the viewers a close-up on each jewel, enhancing every detail of its production and, thereby, providing an unedited perspective and a further insight into Delfina Delettrez's versatile modus operandi.

On one hand, it is always driven by the fascination for the special relationship between micro and macro cosmos and for the juxtapositions between the biological world and technological poesies. On the other, it is constantly aligned with the foundations of Italian artistic and artisanal tradition: technical excellence and creativity, culture and suggestiveness, irony and melancholy and wonder.

Contact/ Antonella Villanova
Address/ Via della Spada 36/R, Palazzo Ricasoli,
Piazza Goldoni 2, Florence, 50123, Italy
Call/ +390556802066
Email/ antonellavillanova@gmail.com
www.antonellavillanova.it

Portrait
Designer/ Delfina Delettrez
Year/ 2012
Materials/ Gold, silver, diamonds, rubies and pearls
Dimensions/ 13.5 × 1 × 8 cm
Courtesy of Lorenzo Michelini

Adamo Ed Eva Earrings
Designer/ Delfina Delettrez
Year/ 2012
Materials/ Gold, peridots and Iolite stones
Dimensions/ 2.5 × 1.57 × 7.5 cm
Courtesy of Delfina Delettrez

Booo/
Eindhoven

Front

Based in Eindhoven, the Netherlands, BOOO is a team of experts from different fields that work in the space between avant-garde design and the consumer market.

In Milan 2012, BOOO presented its first collection of LED bulbs - a light bulb that integrates the function and the aesthetics of a design lamp - created by Nacho Carbonell, Front and Studio Formafantasma.

The BOOO Lab represents BOOO's experimental projects and commissions.

The gallery challenged three of the most cutting-edge design studios to reinvent, in absolute freedom, the concept of a light bulb by investigating unconventional materials and technologies.

The first result of this experimentation is the Surface Tension Lamp designed by the Swedish design studio Front and produced by BOOO in an edition of twenty pieces.

Despite being exclusive works the BOOO Lab represents a continuous investigation towards new and unpredictable uses of innovative technologies.

Contact/ Arjen Heus
Address/ Bloemfonteinstraat 62,
Eindhoven, 5642 EH, Netherlands
Call/ +31622885003
Email/ arjen@booo.nl
www. booo.nl

Surface Tension Lamp
Designer/ Front Design
Year/ 2012
Materials/ Metal, LED and soap
Dimensions/ Various
Courtesy of BOOO Lab

Design Space/
Tel Aviv

Michal Cederbaum
Noam Dover

Along the history of human civilization, pots, pans, vases, bottles and bowls were made and used in a specific context: materials have always been related to a local environment and climate; production techniques were closely linked to folk wisdom, family traditions and industrial developments; and methods of use are associated with social structures and beliefs. Furthermore, vessels have always been part of commercial activity, acting as cultural ambassadors and transferring knowledge between civilizations.

Vessels contain, reflect and reveal culture. They are a manifestation of the link between nature, human needs and the civilized act of "making".

For Design Miami/ 2012, Design Space presents vessels that evolved in light of these ideas. They are produced in limited editions and involve various techniques and methods of production, from hand-made crafts to contemporary technology.

Design Space, directed by Emmy Shahar and Salome Fakiel, was established in 2010 to encourage creative innovation and provide a platform for progressive design and art, featuring both emerging and established artists' work. The gallery is presenting various fields of design, ranging from furniture and industrial products to diverse art exhibitions. Through collaborations with various creative sectors, Design Space produces projects and initiatives, extending its vision internationally.

Noam Dover and Michal Cederbaum initiated their joint studio in 2009. Coming from different fields of design and often working with other artists and designers, their creative dialogue strives to be a broad and multidisciplinary one. Together, their work has so far spanned furniture and hand-made objects, scenography, graphic design, street art and theoretical writing.

The exhibition includes three works in collaborations with Amit Drori (theatre director and designer), Yoav Reches (designer), Tom Tlalim (artist and musician) and Jerome Vernez (video artist).

Contact/ Emmanuella Shahar
Address/ Elifelet 26, Tel Aviv, 66080, Israel
Call/ +972546228764
Email/ emmy@designspace.me
www.designspacetlv.com

Concrete
Designer/ Noam Dover and Michal Cederbaum
Year/ 2012
Materials/ Concrete
Dimensions/ 29.5 × 29.5 × 49 cm
Courtesy of Rami Maymon

Concrete
Designer/ Noam Dover and Michal Cederbaum
Year/ 2012
Materials/ Concrete
Dimensions/ 29.5 × 29.5 × 49 cm
Courtesy of Rami Maymon

Erastudio Apartment-Gallery/ Milan

Gaetano Pesce

Erastudio Apartment-Gallery is a design gallery focusing exclusively on architectural and design works carried out by the most valued and renowned names of the Italian and International architectural scene of the twentieth and twenty-first century.

The gallery is purposely concealed in two private spaces, inside a historic building of the early twentieth century, located in the Brera Design District in Milan.

The first space is an apartment on the third floor and the other one is a building in the courtyard, on the ground floor: the former horse stables. The latter opened during the Fuorisalone 2012, with a site-specific design exhibition by Italian Architect Vincenzo De Cotiis, presenting prototypes and unique pieces exclusively conceived for Erastudio.

The apartment space has been brought back to its original charm after being restored under the supervision of owner Architect Patrizia Tenti. Its pared down walls become a unique scenario, which perfectly suits the works of the architects the gallery represents.

The former stables, the second location of Erastudio Apartment-Gallery, have not been refurbished in order to preserve their authentic look, and will be a temporal platform to be molded according to the philosophy of the works of the represented architects.

The project "America Table" by Architect Gaetano Pesce is a tribute to the United States of America. In fact this table, a unique piece, commemorates the figure Thomas Jefferson who wrote the Declaration of Independence in 1776.

Contact/ Patrizia Tenti
Address/ Via Palermo n. 5, Ground floor & 3rd floor Milan, 20121, Italy
Call/ +390239198515
Email/ patrizia.tenti@erastudio.it
apartmentgallery@erastudio.it
www.erastudio.it

America Table
Designer/ Gaetano Pesce
Year/ 2012
Materials/ Epoxy resin
Dimensions/ 343 × 157 × 75 cm
Courtesy of Erastudio Apartment-Gallery

Mondo Cane/
New York

RO/LU

Mondo Cane was founded in 1994 and since then has been a regular exhibitor at events in New York, Miami and Palm Springs and Los Angeles.In September 2000 Mondo Cane opened its first shop in Chelsea. By 2004 Mondo Cane had outgrown its Chelsea location and decided to move the gallery to 174 Duane Street in Tribeca.

Working with architect William Massie, Mondo Cane was able to create an interesting environment to display their particular vision of the period 1880 to the present. Major designers, architects and artists are represented along with what might be Mondo Cane's strongest point—lesser known and anonymous artisans and designers.

The shop's inventory and design lean toward the unusual and unpredictable.

_____

Contact/ Patrick Parrish
Address/ 174 Duane Street, New York City NY, 10013, US
Call/ +1212 219 9244
Email/ info@mondocane.com
www.mondocane.com

Nature/ Nurture
Designer/ RO/LU
Year/ 2012
Materials/ Walnut treated with brie wax and pink, red and blue Laminate
Dimensions/ 99 × 22 × 122 cm
Courtesy of Mondo Cane

Victor Hunt Designart Dealer/ Brussels

Sylvain Willenz + CIRVA

Victor Hunt Designart Dealer has traded and curated contemporary design since 2008. The gallery's services focus on the search for and investment in prototype, limited and designer's editions from the most remarkable emerging creators.

We offer the designs the industry can't.

Victor Hunt is a branded personality: a progressive alter ego allowing us to customize our relationship with each of our clients.

We understand designart as the gray zone within industrial design, craft, architecture, sculpture and many other art disciplines. We operate as retailers, and as vveditors, depending on the project.

We have a permanent collection on show to offer the fullest possible range of identity-driven work, while also having an ephemeral exhibition space to highlight recent evolutions in the field of contemporary designart.

Based in Brussels with a strong international network and web presence, we answer today's 2.0 habits and curiosity with an extensive image catalogue as well as short documentaries showing the creative processes and personalities behind our collection.

Contact/ Alexis Ryngaert
Address/ Lambert Crickx 16, Brussels, 1070, Belgium
Call/ +3227879957
Email/ victor@victor-hunt.com
www.victor-hunt.com

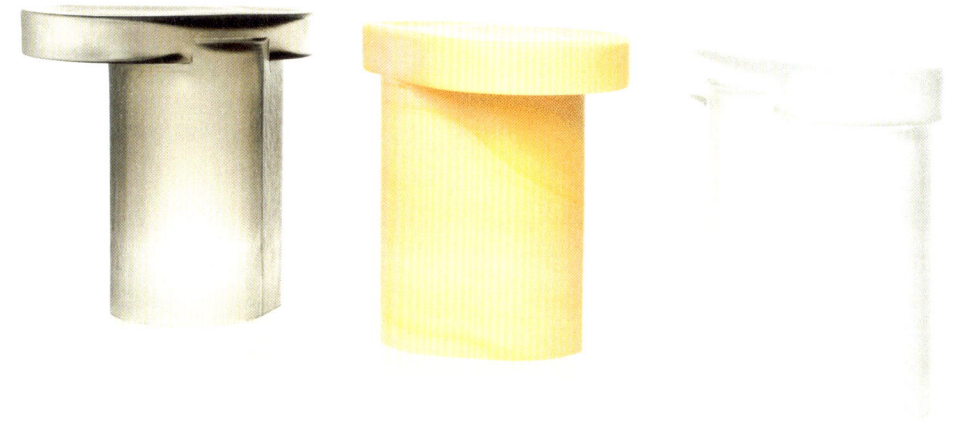

Shift – ensemble of graphite, yellow and clear
Designer/ Sylvain Willenz
Year/ 2012
Materials/ Glass
Dimensions/ Various
Courtesy of Victor Hunt Designart Dealer

Volume Gallery/
Chicago

Snarkitecture

Volume Gallery is an event-based gallery with a specific focus on American design and a strong emphasis placed on emerging contemporary designers.

The gallery releases editions, publications and organizes exhibitions that showcase the work of American designers to regional, national and international audiences. It asks critical questions of what it means to be an American designer in a culture that is rapidly becoming more global, while simultaneously examining the American experience.

Contact/ Claire Warner / Sam Vinz
Address/ 845 West Washington Blvd, Chicago IL, 60607, USA
Call/ +17733684888
Email/ info@wvvolumes.com
www.wvvolumes.com

Split
Designer / Snarkitecture
Year / 2012
Materials / Cast marble
Dimensions / 30 × 30 × 46 cm
Courtesy of Volume Gallery

Pour
Designer / Snarkitecture
Year / 2012
Materials / Oak and marble
Dimensions / 86 × 53 × 46 cm
Courtesy of Volume Gallery

A Z E

AND

E

HT

Design Performance Transformations by Maarten de Ceulaer Presented by Fendi

For the next edition of the ongoing Design Performance program at Design Miami, Fendi invited Belgian designer Maarten de Ceulaer to develop a project that responds to Fendi's visual identity and the brand's legacy of Modernist-inspired patterns and emblems. Maarten was selected for this project because he has demonstrated a remarkable affinity for crafting sophisticated furniture and objects imbued with lyrical, whimsical narrative.

The designer found particular inspiration in Fendi's signature Pequin motif, creating "Transformations" in celebration of Fendi's long heritage of abstract rectilinear and geometric imagery. Throughout the decades, Fendi designers have drawn from the beautiful, groundbreaking work of pioneering design movements such as the Wiener Werkstätte, De Stijl, Futurism, the Bauhaus and Art Deco. Since 1983, Fendi has incorporated striped Pequin materials into many accessory lines, from handbags to luggage. Numerous designs for Fendi furs also feature patterns that evoke the feel of vanguard graphic designs from the 1910s to the 1930s.

For Design Miami/ 2012, Maarten has transformed this repertoire of two-dimensional expression into a three-dimensional installation, exploring the boundaries between hard and soft, natural and man-made, organic and geometric, luxurious and mundane. Converting the idea of a stripe into a physical module based on a piece of lumber, "Transformations" juxtaposes lacquered wood boards and tree stumps with exquisitely handmade leather planks arranged in a variety of eye-catching, multicolored compositions. The result is a total environment that, as whole, becomes a living pattern reminiscent of design work from the early years of Modernism.

The "soft planks" that Maarten developed for this project can be applied wherever additional comfort is desired: the gesture of applying them is as simple as nailing a board to a tree.

FENDI

Maarten de Ceulaeur
Photo/ Nico Neefs

Transformations
Photo/ Nico Neefs

Transformations Tree Trunk for 2 Persons
Photo/ Nico Neefs

Design Miami/ 2012
Design Talks

Design Miami's Design Talks program presents the design world's most compelling current topics, bringing together the creatives, collectors and critics actively influencing design discourse and production.

This December's Design Talks series is dedicated to Design Pioneers, innovators who have worked at the forefront of prominent movements in design history. These Pioneers have crossed the boundaries of design, art, fashion and architecture to cultivate new ways of interpreting material culture and transform the way we view the designed object.

The Design Miami/ 2012 Design Talks take place from 6–7pm on 5.–7. December

BE OPEN Forum

In partnership with BE OPEN, a global initiative to foster innovation and creativity, Design Miami/ launches the BE OPEN Forum. This series of profile talks with advanced thinkers provides a unique portal into the intellectual curiosity of today's design minds.

The BE OPEN Forum takes place from 2–4pm on December 8th.

BEOPEN
CREATIVE THINK TANK

Design Miami/ 2011 Design Talks

R18 Ultra Chair by Clemens Weisshaar and Reed Kram/ for Audi

Clemens Weisshaar and Reed Kram have developed a chair using methods borrowed from the future of automotive manufacturing in collaboration with Audi's Lightweight Design Center. The chair's multi-material space-frame is made from carbon composites, carbon micro-sandwich and high strength aluminium and weighs only 2.2 kg or 77 ounces. The chair embodies Audi's ultra lightweight design credo completely by following strict guidelines to shave off every ounce of excess weight.

The R18 Ultra Chair's genesis incorporates crowd-sourced data acquired through thousands of testing sessions held in Milan during the Salone Internazionale del Mobile in April 2012. This data set was then processed by custom algorithms to optimize the final geometry and construction of the final object accordingly.

At Design Miami/ the chair's designers and engineers are giving visitors an intimate insight into their studios and laboratories, displaying drawings, samples, models, mock-ups, moulds and prototypes from the various stages in the development process including an industrial welding robot and the chair's namesake, the 24h of Le Mans winning R18 Ultra race car.

Audi
Vorsprung durch Technik

R18 Ultra Chair
Designers/ Clemens Weisshaar and Reed Kram
Materials/ Cardboard Model Scale 1:1
Photography/ Frank Stolle

PARHELIA by Asif Khan/
for Swarovski Crystal Palace

Swarovski is pleased to welcome Asif Khan as this year's designer for Swarovski Crystal Palace. At Design Miami/ 2012, Khan will present Parhelia, an immersive installation that explores the relationship between crystal, light, nature, and architecture.

"Parhelia is an experiment that begins at the crossroads of architecture and nature," says Khan. "I was first inspired by the atmospheric and optical properties of the sky in northern latitudes and with the idea of transporting these elements to another, contrasting environment. The installation is also about bringing together architecture, crystals, light, and space."

Founded in 2007, Asif Khan Ltd. is an award-winning architecture practice based in London with a design approach based on experimentation, collaboration, and close dialogue with clients. The designer's work spans the disciplines of architecture, furniture, and industrial design while combining them in new and unexpected ways.

Khan studied for his architecture degree at the Bartlett School UCL and graduated in 2004 with honors. Upon graduation, he was featured in The Architects' Journal and awarded a full scholarship to attend the Architectural Association in London. In 2007, Building Design magazine profiled him as one of the 10 best graduating architects in the United Kingdom.

In 2010, Khan earned a prestigious 'Designer in Residence' slot at the Design Museum London – the first architect ever to be given that honor. Khan was awarded 'Designer of the Future' by Design Miami/ in 2011, and featured in the New York Times as one of five designers to watch in 2011. In 2012, Khan went on to design Coca-Cola's pavilion at the London 2012 Olympic Games.

"For ten years, Swarovski Crystal Palace has been a revolutionary project aimed at creating signature interpretations of light and design. Swarovski commissioned Asif Khan to create a concept for Design Miami/ that is inspired by nature while incorporating crystal in an instrumental way in his creation," says Nadja Swarovski, Member of the Executive Board, Swarovski Crystal Business.

SWAROVSKI CRYSTAL PALACE

Halo display in the Czech mountains
Photographer/ Jirí Žujic
Year/ ©2008

LOST TIME by Glithero/
Presented by
Champagne Perrier-Jouët

In honor of Emile Gallé's iconic bottle design for Belle Époque cuvée , Perrier-Jouët has invited London-based design studio Glithero to create an installation inspired by the curvilinear forms and natural motifs of the Art Nouveau movement.

The result is Lost Time (Temps Perdu), an ode to the work of Art Nouveau architect Antoni Gaudi. In designing his Sagrada Familia Church in Barcelona, Gaudi's goal was to find nature's purest, most perfect curves. To achieve this, he created upside-down architectural models composed of a multitude of weighted strings that draped from the ceiling, relying on the natural force of gravity to define the dynamic arcs of his stunning masterwork.

Lost Time (Temps Perdu) borrows Gaudi's model-making technique to create an experiential environment that plays with perception. Upon entering the installation, the darkness envelops the viewer; within the dim light, one can discern thousands of suspended, arching beads that stretch downward toward a mirror-like pond below. The water multiplies and inverts the curving forms, challenging the viewer to distinguish the real from the replica; meanwhile, the restricted lighting produces a feeling of time frozen in a moment of reflection.

Tim Simpson and Sarah van Gameren, Glithero

Lost Time

Drift Pavillion
Designed by Snarkitecture

An entrance pavilion for Design Miami/ 2012, Drift creates an unexpected moment within the context of the familiar white vinyl tent, reformulating the material to create a floating environment. Inflated tubes are bundled together to create a topographical landscape in suspension: an ascending mountain above and an excavated cavern below. These long cylinders are arranged vertically to infill the area of the entrance courtyard, and then lifted to create areas of circulation and rest for the visitors entering and exiting the structure.

Filtered light passes between the tubes of the inverted landscape creating a space both interactive and contemplative. Apertures in the canopy above frame views of the Miami sky and allow natural light and fresh air into the interior. The lightness of the floating tubes underscores the mass of the enormous installation, visible from a distance of several blocks. Drift identifies the entrance courtyard as a site of activity and design. The rising landscape becomes a beacon for visitors approaching Design Miami/ while the excavated cavern presents a moment of exploration before entering the fair.

Snarkitecture is a collaborative practice operating in territories between the disciplines of art and architecture. Working within existing spaces or in collaboration with other artists and designers, the practice focuses on the investigation of structure, material and program and how these elements can be manipulated to serve new and imaginative purposes. Searching for sites within architecture with the possibility for confusion or misuse, Snarkitecture aims to make architecture perform the unexpected.

Address/ 60 Box Street, Brooklyn NY, 11222, USA
Call/ +17183051560
Email/ info@snarkitecture.com
www.snarkitecture.com

Drift, Snarkitecture

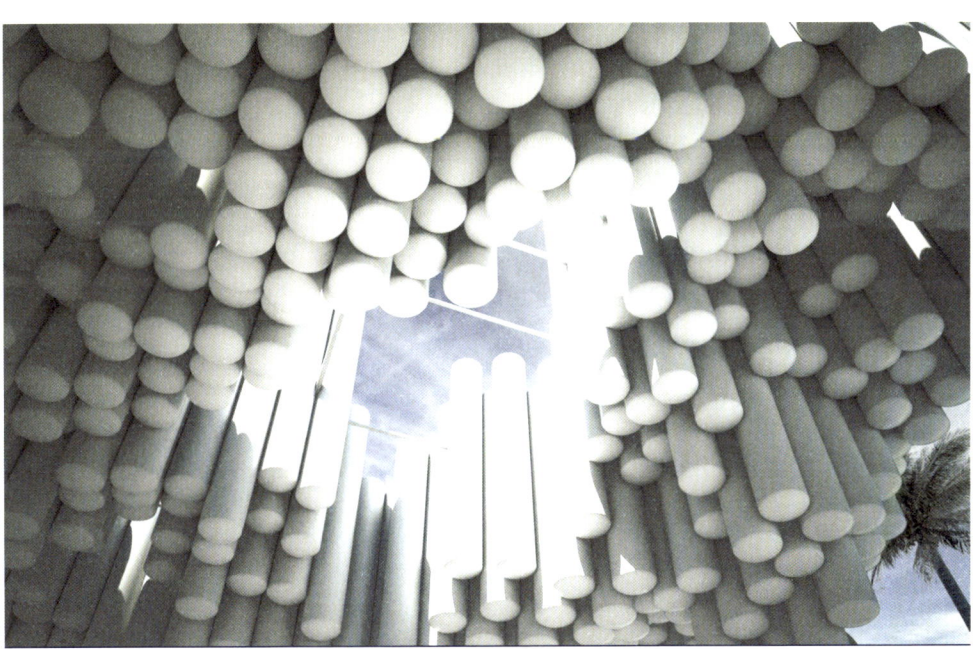

Drift, Snarkitecture

ARTBOOK & The Shop at Cooper-Hewitt/

For Design Miami/ 2012, America's premiere art and design bookseller, ARTBOOK | D.A.P., teams up with The Shop at Cooper-Hewitt, National Design Museum, Smithsonian Institution—the only museum in the nation devoted exclusively to historic and contemporary design—to offer a selection of intriguing and collectible books and objects related to the fair.

ARTBOOK presents new and classic books on important twentieth century designers, design movements and trends in architectural thinking by the world's greatest art and design publishers, as well as the very first Design Miami/ Library: a curated set of books representing the galleries and designers on view at the 2012 fair.

The Shop at Cooper-Hewitt presents a selection of works by established and emerging designers that will surprise, delight and inspire. The diverse product mix boasts a wide selection of limited-edition works by contemporary designers and exclusive items that relate to both Design Miami/ and the Museum's extensive permanent collections.

Contact/ ARTBOOK | D.A.P.
Address/ 155 Avenue of the Americas, 2nd floor, New York, NY 10013, USA
Call/ +2126271999
Email/ curatorial@artbook.com
www.artbook.com

Contact/ The Shop At Cooper-Hewitt
Call/ +7183843092
Email/ cooperhewittshop@si.edu
www.shop.cooperhewitt.org

Photograph by Matthew Sandager

Architecture for Dogs
Founded by Imprint Lab
in conjunction with
Kenya Hara

Architecture for Dogs is a new concept and commercial company founded by Imprint Lab in conjunction with Kenya Hara, Tokyo-based designer, curator, educator, and Artistic Director for MUJI. For his latest project, Hara has assigned twelve world-renowned architects and designers each a breed of dog for which to design an architectural structure suited to that particular breed's characteristics, temperament, health and living conditions.

Making its worldwide debut in Miami as part of the Design Miami/ Design Satellite program, the exhibition, designed and curated by Hara, will feature twelve designs: Kenya Hara (Teacup Poodle); Atelier Bow-Wow (Dachshund); Shigeru Ban (Papillion); Sou Fujimoto (Boston Terrier); Konstantin Grcic (Poodle); Hara Design Institute (Japanese Terrier); Toyo Ito (Shiba); Kengo Kuma (Pug); MVRDV (Beagle); Hiroshi Naito (Spitz); Reiser + Umemoto (Chihuahua); Kazuyo Sejima (Bichon Frise); and Torafu (Jack Russell Terrier).

The recently launched website, ArchitectureForDogs.com, was designed by Yugo Nakamura, a Tokyo-based graphic and interactive designer who has worked extensively with Uniqlo and Louis Vuitton, among others. The site features free downloadable blueprints of every design in the collection, thereby allowing anyone anywhere in the world the ability to build each Architecture for Dogs structure free of charge. Full instructions on materials and build out, as well as instructional videos on the site encourage the highly interactive element of Hara's concept. After building the designs, visitors to the site are encouraged to upload their own versions of each structure onto the Architecture for Dogs website or submit their own design ideas.

After Architecture for Dog's Miami debut, the concept will travel to different locations throughout the world before closing with an exhibition in Tokyo's Toto Gallery in October 2013. A final book on the project, tracing the trajectory of the concept from Miami to Tokyo, will be published in conjunction with the Toto Gallery exhibition.

ARCHITECTURE FOR DOGS

Address/ Imprint Venture Lab, 555 E. Ocean Blvd. 9 FL, Long Beach CA, 90802, USA
Email/ info@architecturefordogs.com
www.architecturefordogs.com

D-Tunnel by Kenya Hara for Teacup Poodle
Courtesy of Hiroshi Yoda

Design Miami/ Scent
Designed by 12.29

12.29 New York I Paris is celebrating its fourth year in partnership with Design Miami/. The Design Miami/ scent that blows through the fair was designed by 12.29 in collaboration with the Design Miami/ team to symbolize the electric energy of Miami and the creative intensity of the design world.

In a world where branding is everything and everyone is trying to break through, Samantha and Dawn Goldworm of 12.29 have taken an innovative spin by creating an olfactive branding company that designs custom scents for retail and corporate environments, hospitality venues, special events and private homes. 12.29's point of differentiation is the ability to create a scent designed specifically for the brand identity.

Design and scent are interrelated and codependent on one another. Both mediums express an emotional aesthetic, create a promise and deliver a dream. While most brands are familiar with design aesthetic, auditory, touch and taste cues, almost no brands have exploited olfaction as a message.

Scent is the future of design.

12.29 is a company that creates a scent for your brand, a scent for your home and a scent for your life.

12.29 New York / Paris
Email/ info@1229.com
www.1229.com

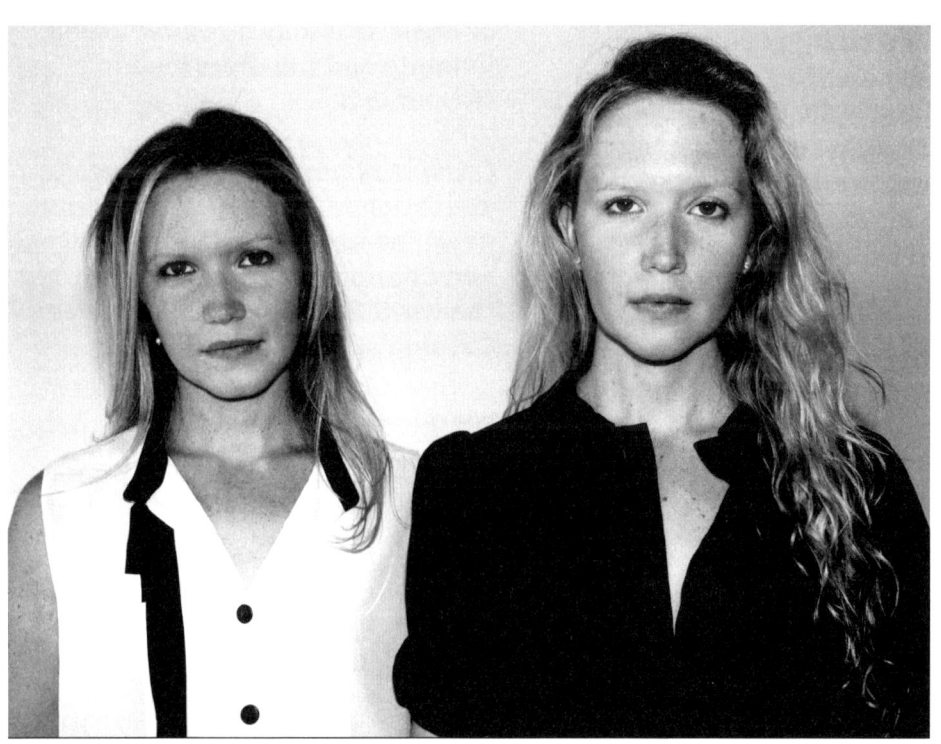

Courtesy of Olivier Zahm

Le Corbusier/
The Interior of the Cabanon Le Corbusier 1952 – Cassina Reconstruction 2006

Cassina, in collaboration with the Le Corbusier Foundation, is proud to present the first U.S. exhibition of Le Corbusier: The Interior of the Cabanon, Le Corbusier 1952 – Cassina Reconstruction 2006. This highly anticipated exhibit will take place at the Cassina Miami showroom during Design Miami 2012, running from December 6, 2012 until January 12, 2013.

The exhibition features the authentic reconstruction of the actual interior of the Cabanon, which Le Corbusier planned and built in 1952 for his holidays in Cap-Martin, France. The Cabanon is an apparently unpretentious sea-side hut, comprising a remarkable example of significant micro-architecture. The Cabanon will be reconstructed in the Cassina Miami showroom. Jean-Louis Cohen, a renowned Le Corbusier scholar and professor of architecture at New York University, will curate the exhibition.

Continuing its in-depth research into the work of the great masters of architecture, contemporary Italian furniture brand Cassina has nurtured this project, and presents it today with the aim of divulging greater knowledge of Le Corbusier's architectural values and the promotion of cultural initiatives. Cassina is the only company with the exclusive worldwide rights to reproduce all products by Le Corbusier, Pierre Jeanneret and Charlotte Perriand, part of the Cassina I Maestri Collection.

The Cabanon conceals a treasured example of architecture by Le Corbusier, who intended to assign its principal architectural importance only to the interior of the construction. The construction reveals a rich, logical and harmonious composition of meaningful resolutions, notwithstanding the more than modest dimensions. It first and foremost teaches us that the problem of the home implies the study of quality choices rather than astonishing details or show. It also reminds us that the ultimate deciding factor in a completed building – extravagant or basic as it may be – is whoever inhabits and transfers human fervour in it.

Cassina Miami will also showcase a collection of Le Corbusier furniture designed together with Pierre Jenneret and Charlotte Perriand highlighting the veritable relationship between Cassina and Le Corbusier.

www.poltronafraumiami.net

December 6, 2012 – January 12, 2013
Address/ Cassina Miami, 3800 NE Miami Court, Miami Design District
Call/ 305-576-3636

Le Corbusier
Roquebrune-Cap-Martin: Cabanon
© FLC/SIAE L3(5)5

Reconstruction Interior of Le Corbusier's Cabanon
Cassina 2006

Designer of The Year 2012

Acconci Studio
Design Miami/
Designer of The Year 2012

Each December, the Design Miami/ Designer of the Year Award recognizes an internationally renowned designer or studio that has made a mark on design history, pushing the boundaries of the discipline through a singularly innovative and influential vision. This year, Design Miami/ is proud to recognize Acconci Studio.

Vito Acconci founded the architecture and design collaborative Acconci Studio in 1988 as the next evolution of his rich and varied creative practice, which began in the 1960s with a focus on concrete poetry and continued through the '70s and '80s with a genre-defining body of work in performance and conceptual art. The trajectory of his career demonstrates an acute and steadfast interest in generating unexpected and intense interactions, in actively engaging both people and public places to explore the spectrum of human response. The architectural projects produced by Acconci Studio carry forward this commitment, comprising fluid and shifting spaces and objects aimed at encouraging out-of the-ordinary communal experiences.

Acconci Studio's boundary-defying approach draws on and intermingles the conceptual basis of Vito's earlier work, employing art-grounded ideas to "thicken the plot," in the artist's words. Yet, Acconci Studio is dedicated to production in the realms of architecture and design because this where there is the greatest possibility to impact everyday living, to surprise, challenge and enchant people as they go about their lives. The comingling of material and ideas to expand the definition of function and to uncover higher purposes for our built environment positions Acconci Studio at the vanguard of design discourse today.

Vito Acconci in the Miami Design District
Photo/ Gesi Schilling

Screens for a Walkway
Location/ Shibuya Station, Tokyo
Year/ 2000

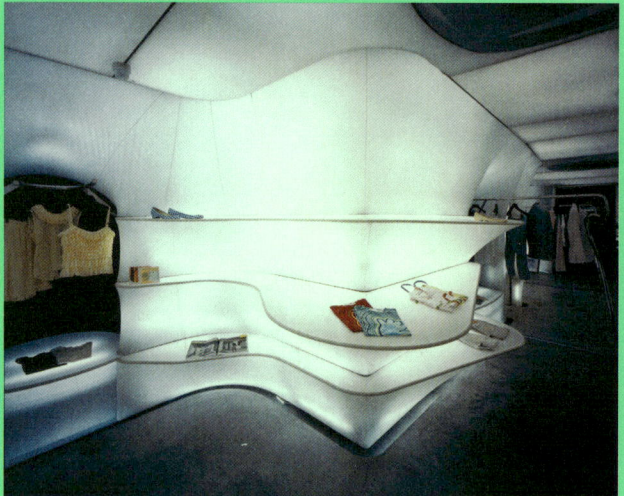

United Bamboo Store
Location/ Tokyo
Year/ 2003

Umbruffla
Year/ 2005

Lobby for The Time Being
Location/ The Bronx
Year/ 2010

Roof Like a Liquid Flung Over the Plaza
Location/ Memphis
Year/ 2005

Waterfall Out and In
Location/ Brooklyn
Year/ 2010

Fence on the Loose
Location/ Toronto
Year/ 2012

Waterfall Out and In
Location/ Brooklyn
Year/ 2010

Mur Island
Location/ Graz
Year/ 2003

Vito Acconci
Photo/ Gesi Schilling

Design Miami/
Designer of The Year
Commission

The Design Miami/ Designer of the Year Award grants each winner a commission to create a large-scale work. Over the years, Design Miami/ has seized opportunities to activate the award as a means to "give back" to the Miami community. Previous examples include the fence that Marc Newson designed for the Design and Architecture Senior High in the Miami Design District, and Konstantin Grcic's Netscape seating structure donated to Miami Art Museum to be used in the public space of the new Herzog & de Meuron building. Moving forward, a permanent and public installation of the Designer of the Year commission will be an integral and unconditional goal of the program. Acconci Studio's collaborative and interactive mission is ideally suited to this kind of community-enhancing brief.

For this year's commission, Acconci Studio will produce a climbing-playing structure to be permanently installed in the Miami Design District by 2014. Klein-Bottle Playground, as the structure is called, was originally developed for the humanitarian "Art for the World" program, as part of a touring exhibition of experimental recreational equipment and toys for refugee children. Acconci Studio's contribution was inspired by the German mathematician Felix Klein, who expanded the concept of a Moebius strip into a structure – a "Klein Bottle" – in which there is no identifiable "inside" or "outside," as one surface flows continuously into the other. Acconci Studio has transformed this mathematical construct into a playground, in which a series of tubes extend out from and into a central sphere, such that children can climb in, through and on top. The installation of Acconci Studio's Klein-Bottle Playground in the Miami Design District will provide the first public area in the neighborhood dedicated to children.

During Design Miami/ 2012, an exhibition of Acconci Studio work will be open to the public in the Miami Design District from December 4th through the 9th.

This project has been realized with the support of Miami Design District.

MIAMI
DESIGN
DISTRICT

Wave a Wall
Location/ West 8th Subway Station, New York
Year/ 2006

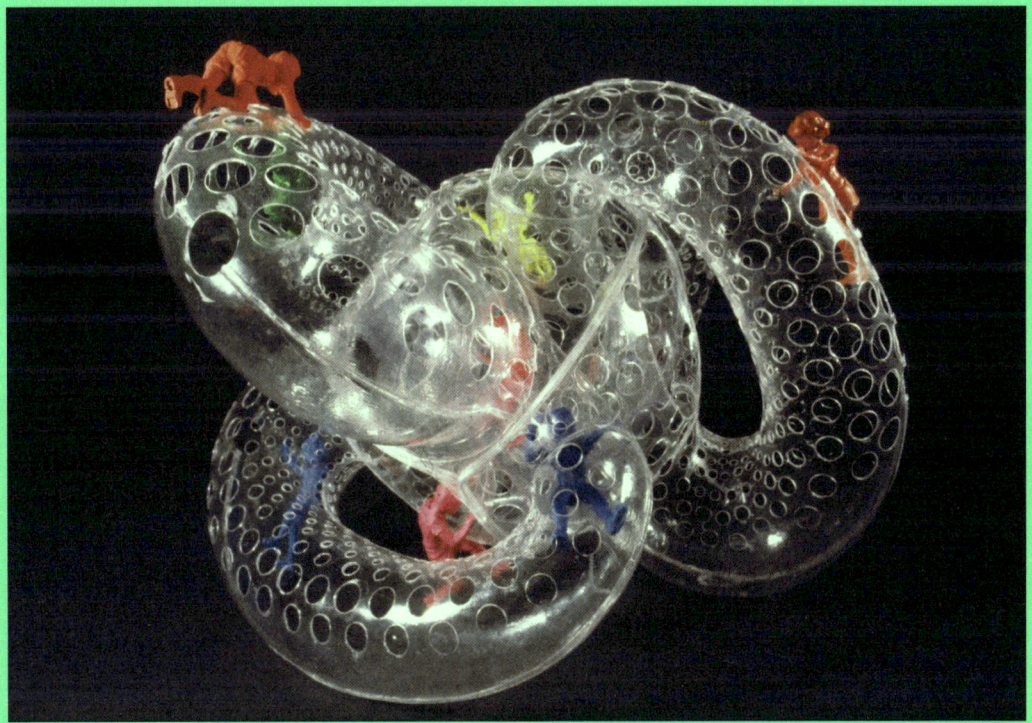

Klein-Bottle Playground
Year/ 2000

Roof Like a Liquid Flung Over a Plaza
Location/ Memphis
Year/ 2005

Screens for a Walkway
Location/ Shibuya Station, Tokyo
Year/ 2000

Umbruffla
Year/ 2005

Mur Island
Location/ Graz
Year/ 2003

Fence on the Loose
Location/ Toronto
Year/ 2012

About the Studio

Acconci Studio's design & architecture comes from another direction, from Vito Acconci's backgrounds in writing and art. His poems in the late 60's treated language as matter (words to look at rather than through) and the page as a field to travel over; his performances in the early 70's helped shift art from object to interaction between art-doer and viewer; later in the 70's, his installations turned viewers into participants; in the early 80's, his architectural-units could be transformed by users. By the late 80's his work crossed over and he formed Acconci Studio, a design firm that mixes poetry and geometry, computer-scripting and sentence-structure, narrative and biology, chemistry and social-science.

The Studio uses computers to give form to thinking; they use forms to find ideas. They make not nodes so much as circulation-routes; they design time as much as space. Their design starts with clothing and ends with vehicles – in between, they design buildings that slip into landscape and vice versa; they make spaces fluid, changeable and portable; they make architecture subservient to people and not vice versa; they anticipate cities on the move. Built in the last decade is, in Graz, a person-made island where a bowl (the theater) twists into a playground on its way to becoming a dome (the restaurant). Being built now, in Indianapolis, is an interactive tunnel through a building where pedestrians and cyclists set off lights that swarm around them like fireflies.

Open Book Store
Location/ Armory Show, New York
Year/ 2007

Wave a Wall
Location/ West 8th Street Subway Station, New York
Year/ 2006

A Skate Park That Glides The Land & Drops Into The Sea
Location/ San Juan
Year/ 2004

Open Book Store, Armory Show
Location/ New York
Year/ 2007

Vito Acconci
Photo/ Gesi Schilling

Swarm Street
Location/ Indianapolis
Year/ 2012

Roof Like a Liquid Flung Over a Plaza
Location/ Memphis
Year/ 2005

Acknowledgements

Design Miami/ is made possible through the generous support of Dacra, a creative real estate company specializing in innovative projects combining architecture, art, design and fashion.

Design Miami/ is partnered with MCH Group

Design Miami/ wishes to express enthusiastic appreciation for our sponsors

Exclusive Automotive Sponsor

Main Sponsor

SWAROVSKI CRYSTAL PALACE

Design Performance

FENDI

Exclusive Champagne Sponsor

Collectors Lounge Host

REGALIA
Limited Edition Living

Collectors Lounge Design

Cassina

Furniture Sponsor

cappellini

Alias

Designer of the Year Award Partner

MIAMI DESIGN DISTRICT

Online Partner

ARTSY

BE OPEN Forum

Museum Partners

bassmuseum of art

 Smithsonian
Cooper-Hewitt, National Design Museum

Miami Art Museum
Reopening as the Pérez Art Museum Miami
in downtown Miami's Museum Park fall 2013

MUSEUM OF CONTEMPORARY ART NORTH MIAMI

Smithsonian
Archives of American Art

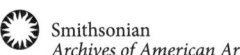
WOLFSONIANFIU

Design Provider/ Supporter

evian.

Hospitality Partner

Design Miami/ wishes to thank the Cities of Miami Beach and Basel

MIAMIBEACH

Basel
www.basel.ch

Special Thanks
Special Thanks to/ Art Basel
Annette Schönholzer, Director/
Marc Spiegler, Director and the Art Basel Team

Board of Directors
René Kamm/ Craig Robins

Executive Board
Marianne Goebl/ Thomas Hochuli/ René Kamm/
Craig Robins/ Annette Schönholzer/ Anna Williams

Gallery Committee
Suzanne Demisch/ Pierre Marie Giraud/
Clémence & Didier Krzentowski/ Laurence & Patrick Seguin

Vetting Committee
Simon Andrews/ Al Eiber/ Ulrich Fiedler/
François Laffanour

Designer of the Year
Acconci Studio

Design Miami/ also wishes to thank the local
authorities for their support

City of Miami Beach Mayor
Matti Herrera Bower

Vice Mayor
Jorge Exposito

City Manager
Kathie G. Brooks

Assistant City Manager
Jorge Gomez

Acting Assistant City Manager
Max Sklar

Commissioners
Michael Gongora/ Jerry Libbin/ Edward L. Tobin/
Deede Weithorn/ Jonah Wolfson

Department of Tourism and Cultural Development
Graham Winick/ Linette Nodarse

City of Miami Beach Cultural Arts Council
City of Miami Beach Police Department
City of Miami Beach Fire Department

Acknowledgements with thanks
Debbie Ahn/ Audra Asencio/ Paul Austin/ Silvia Barisione/
Elena Baturina/ Caroline Baumann/ Tracy Belcher/
Kristi Blake/ Larissa Braun/ Ibiayi Briggs /
Axelle de Buffévent/ Tracey Robertson Carter/
Carter Cleveland/ Isabel Chattas/ Tiffany Chestler/
Nicholas Christopher/ Katherine Cocke/ Thom Collins/
Silvia Cubiña/ Sebastian Cwilich/ Melina De Stefano/
Amy Dollamore/ Grace Duncan/ Stéphanie Durroux/
Aldo Faetti/ Silvia Fendi/ George Fleck/
Jacqueline Fletcher/ Angella Forbes/ Patrick Foret/
Alexander Galan/ Yamila Garayzer/ Alexandra Gilbert /
Monica Gioia/ Bob Goodman/ Dawn Goldworm/
Samantha Goldworm/ Mary Gomez/ Austin Harrelson/
Sarah Harrelson/ David Holtzman/ Mayda Horstmann/
Anthony Ingham/ Anne Ishii/ Samuel Keller/ Mateo Kries/
Amy Lau/ Cathy Leff/ Tara Levy/ John Lin/
George Lindemann/ Andrea Lipps/ Rodrigo Londono/
Marco Lucarelli/ Christy MacLear/ Nadine Marti/
Cara McCarty/ Stéphanie Mingham/ Cristiana Monfardini/
Lou Montello/ Chris Moorby/ Maria Morosova/
Bernhard Neumann/ Sascha Nikitin/ Sandra Novas/
Tania Nudelman/ Reiner Packeiser/ Ben Parker/
Konstantin Polyanichev/ Demetra J. Prattas/ Ian Prentice/
Meire Ramos/ Stefanie Reed/ Katrin Regler/
Lucie Simon-Rehm/ Cory Reynolds/ Megan Riley/
Maria Ruiz/ Jackie Sayet/ Michael Schwartz/
Diana Shtreykher/ Eve Skillicorn/ Stefan Sielaff/
Maria Sole Henny/ Kathrin Speidel/ Jessica Spirer/
Rupert Stadler/ Leann Standish/ Francis Sultana/
Nadja Swarovski/ Gennady Terebkov/ Bryan Terzi/
Michael Tiedy/ Stefano Tonchi/ Brooke Travis/
Mark Turkel/ Kevin Venger/ Alistair Webb/ Laura Wietfeld/
Pharrell Williams/ Denise Wilson/ Donald Worth/
Diane von Furstenberg/ Alexander Von Vegesack/
Marc Zehntner

Design Miami/ Organization

Principal
Craig Robins

Chief Operating Officer
Steven Gretenstein

Co-Founder
Ambra Medda

Vice President
Anna Williams

Director
Marianne Goebl

Director of Marketing
Kapila Chase

Director of Exhibitions
Alexandra Cunningham

Director of External Relations
Ashlee Harrison

Sponsor & VIP Relations
Brittany Silver

Exhibition Coordinator
Brandon Grom

Marketing Coordinator
Nicole Irizarry

Logistics Director
Ty Bassett

Operations Manager
Joanne Green

Logistics Manager
Kevin Perkins

Logistics Coordinator
Komal Kehar

Operations Coordinator
Jenna Harcher

Project Coordinator
Stephanie Lobato

Curatorial Consultant
Wava Carpenter

General Counsel
Linda Ebin/ Patrick Graber

Director of Finance & Administration
Jon Levin

Project Accounting
Carrie Acosta/ Marcia Katz/ Marisel Rodriguez

Sponsorship & Communications
Ainsworth Associates/ Susan Ainsworth, President

Public Relations
Camron PR/ Judy Dobias, Managing Director/
Adnan Abbasi/ Valentina Giani/ Lisa Mcmillan/
Sarah Natkins/ Doug Roche/ James Hart

Project Architects
Aranda\Lasch/ Ben Aranda/ Chris Lasch

Identity, Collateral & Signage
MadeThought

Catering
Michael's Genuine Food & Drink

Thank you for your visit
to Design Miami/ 2012

See you in Basel
/10/ June/ Preview Day
/11/12/13/14/15/16 /
June 2013

The Global Forum
For Design

Design/
Miami/
   /Basel

Namesake
The Le Mans winning R18 racecar is both source of inspiration as well as a the namesake for the R18 Ultra Chair.

Design Development
Threedimensional computer models and physical cardboard models are used to iteratively visualize the evolution of the chair.

Exclusive Automotive Sponsor of Design Miami/

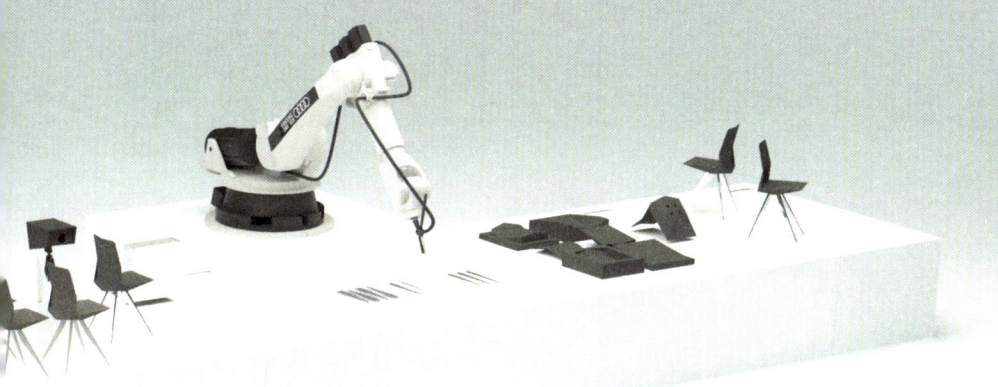

The Chair
The R18 Ultra Chair combines Audi`s lightweight design credo in a 2200g light piece of furniture.

Ultra: Carbon Fibre
The latest carbon composite materials are used for the chair`s seat shell.

Ultra: Aluminium
The chair`s legs are folded sheet alumium, welded by an industrial robot.

Public Beta
A prototype version of the chair was fitted out with sensors and tested by visitors.

R18 Ultra Chair
designed by Clemens Weisshaar
and Reed Kram

Vorsprung durch Technik **Audi**

Get Cultured.

Now Available Quarterly

SWAROVSKI CRYSTAL PALACE

PROUD SPONSOR OF DESIGN MIAMI/ 2012
IRIS BY FREDRIKSON STALLARD FOR SWAROVSKI CRYSTAL PALACE

WWW.BRAND.SWAROVSKI.COM

FENDI

Disegno.

No.3

Shigeru Ban
Nelly Ben Hayoun
Maria Blaisse
Design Erotica
Olafur Eliasson
Eley Kishimoto
The Fold
Orhan Pamuk
Victor Papanek
Julie Richoz

UK £12
EU €15
US $25

03 >
9 772048 777008

NOW BRINGS YOU DAILY DESIGN NEWS ON
disegnodaily.com

PLEASE VISIT "LOST TIME/TEMPS PERDU" BY GLITHERO AT DESIGN MIAMI/ BOOTH S/02

PLEASE ENJOY OUR FINE WINES RESPONSIBLY

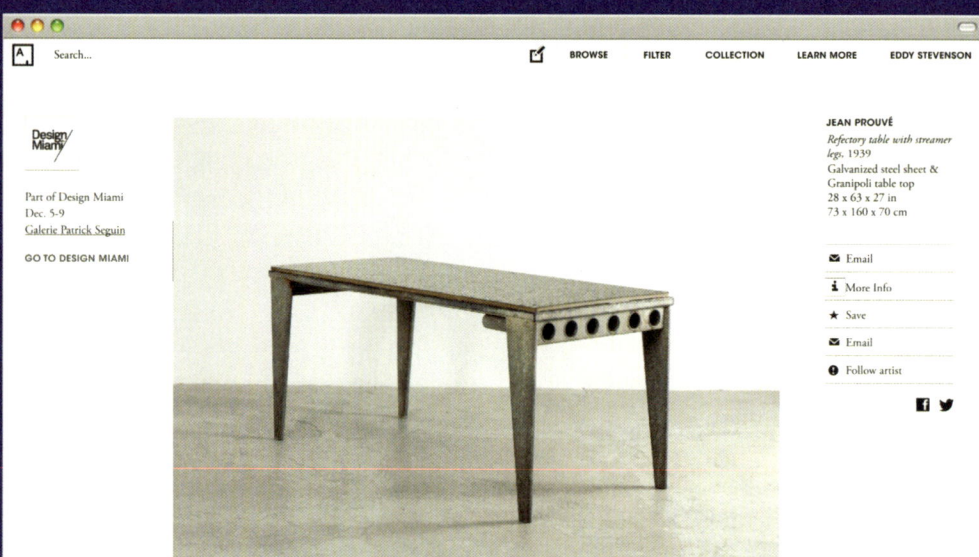

PIN–UP

ISSUE 13
FALL WINTER 2012/13

OUT

Featuring
JEANNE GANG, PETER SHIRE,
H.R. GIGER, OSCAR TUAZON
PHILIPPE MALOUIN, ERWIN WURM

NOW

JURGEN BEY, PAUL RUDOLPH,
LEONG LEONG plus a
48-PAGE NEW YORK CITY SPECIAL

www.pinupmagazine.org

QVEST

a MAGAZIN about *fashion,*
culture *& attitude*

facebook.com/qvest.magazine
iPad-App: otheredition.com/qvest

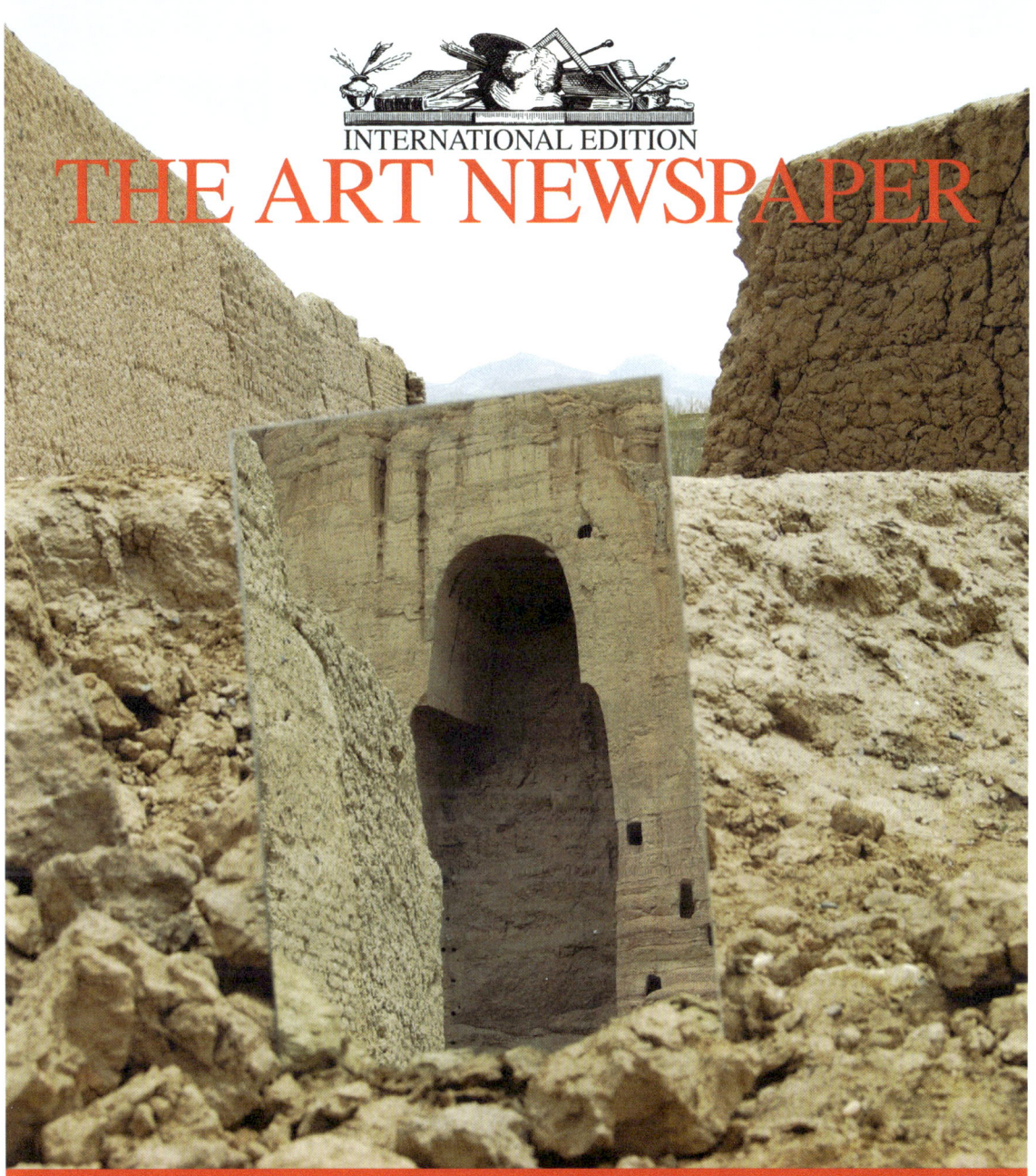

INTERNATIONAL EDITION

THE ART NEWSPAPER

Covering all the news on the art world from Antiquity to Contemporary

WWW.THEARTNEWSPAPER.COM

William Cobbing, *Bamiyan Mirror Series 215*, Afghanistan, 2009 (detail)

TURON TRAVEL, INC.

2 Wooster Street, SoHo, New York, 10013
212-925-5453 / 800-952-7646
www.turontravel.com

SM

Serving the Art World Since 1979

Art Fairs & Biennales
Quarterly eDirectory
Museum Groups & Art Specialist Tours

VISUAL ART
MUSIC
LITERATURE

MR

THE MIAMI RAIL

www.miamirail.org

The Miami Rail is made possible with the generous support of the John S. & James L. knight Foundation

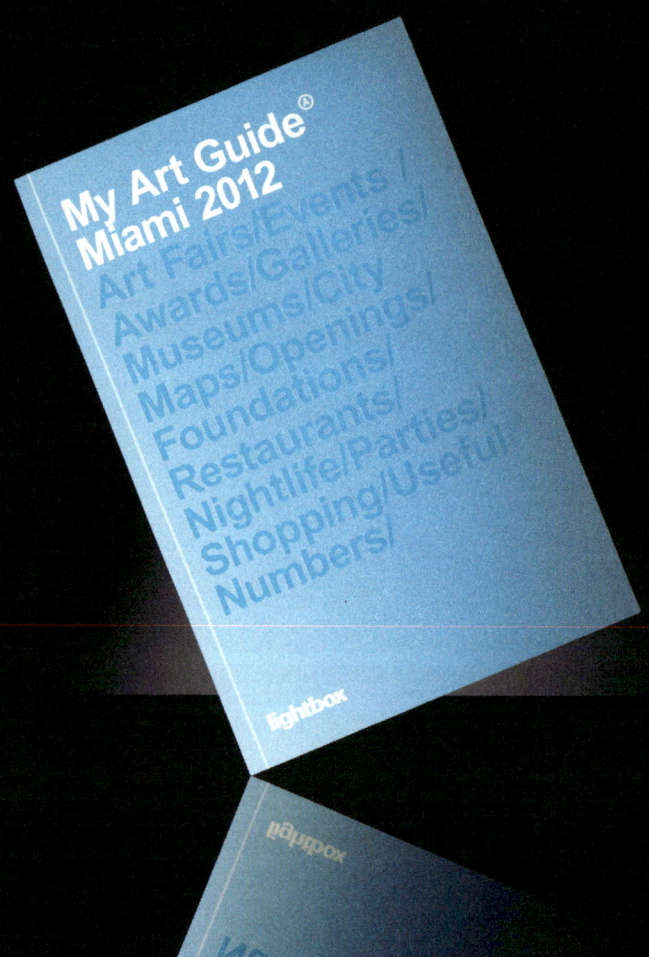

www.atcasa.it

CASE DA ABITARE

Interiors, Design & Living

ABITARE

*Reading the designed environment:
architecture, design, art and communication*

THE SOURCE.

The dynamic destination for
design, art, luxury and food

38th to 41st Streets between
NE 2nd Avenue and N Miami Avenue
Miami, FL 33137
Phone 305.722.7100
miamidesigndistrict.net

Store hours 10am — 7pm
$3 Valet Parking

WHERE
ART
HAPPENS

MIAMI

WHERE
FOOD
HAPPENS

ADAMAR FINE ARTS
AREVALO GALLERY
ART FUSION GALLERY
CRAIG ROBINS ART
COLLECTION
DE LA CRUZ COLLECTION
CONTEMPORARY ART SPACE
ELASTIKA BY ZAHA HADID
ETRA FINE ART
HAITIAN HERITAGE MUSEUM
KIDS BY ROBERTO BEHAR
& ROSARIO MARQUARDT
LOCUST PROJECTS
MARKOWICZ FINE ART
MICHAEL JON GALLERY
OLIVER SANCHEZ STUDIO
PRIMARY PROJECTS
101/EXHIBIT
DASH FENCE BY MARC NEWSON

CRUMB ON PARCHMENT
EGG & DART
HARRY'S PIZZERIA
MANDOLIN AEGEAN BISTRO
MC KITCHEN
MICHAEL'S GENUINE FOOD & DRINK
OAK TAVERN
ORANGE CAFÉ
SOUTH STREET

WHERE
LUXURY
HAPPENS

WHERE
DESIGN
HAPPENS

AGNONA
ANYA PONOROVSKAYA
APT 606
CARTIER
CÉLINE
CHRISTIAN LOUBOUTIN
DIOR HOMME
EMILIO PUCCI COMING SOON
EN AVANCE
INGLOT MIAMI
I ON THE DISTRICT
LOUIS VUITTON
MAISON MARTIN MARGIELA
MARNI
PRADA
SEBASTIEN JAMES
SCOTCH & SODA
TURCHIN LOVE
& LIGHT COLLECTION

ADRIANA HOYOS
ARMANI CASA
ALESSI
BISAZZA
BULTHAUP
CAPPELLINI
DRIADE
DESIGN WITHIN REACH
FENDI CASA
FLOS
HOLLY HUNT
JANUS ET CIE
JONATHAN ADLER
KARTELL
LIGNE ROSET
LUMINAIRE LAB
MADINITALY
MAXALTO
MOROSO
NIBA HOME
ORNARE
POLIFORM
POLTRONA FRAU
SPAZIO DI CASA
TEAM 7
THE RUG COMPANY
VITRA
WATERWORKS
ZANOTTA

DESIGN

DISTRICT

MIAMI
DESIGN
DISTRICT

Design/
Miami/ has launched a new
blog for news from the fair,
design writing,
market commentary,
Q A interviews, exhibition
highlights and more.
Follow Design Log for
exclusive coverage
of Design Miami/ 2012's
gallery shows, award
commissions, design talks
and events.

Designmiamilog.com